FREIDA BAILEY

THE 21 LAWS OF LEADERSHIP SUCCESS

Master Proven Principles to Influence, Inspire, and Lead Effectively

Copyright © 2024 by FREIDA BAILEY

All rights reserved. No part of this publication may be reproduced, stored or transmitted in any form or by any means, electronic, mechanical, photocopying, recording, scanning, or otherwise without written permission from the publisher. It is illegal to copy this book, post it to a website, or distribute it by any other means without permission.

FREIDA BAILEY asserts the moral right to be identified as the author of this work.

First edition

This book was professionally typeset on Reedsy.
Find out more at reedsy.com

Contents

Introduction vi

I Part 1: The Foundation of Leadership

1 Chapter 1: The Law of Influence 3
   Leadership Defined by Influence, Not Title 3
2 Chapter 2: The Law of Connection 7
   Connecting Emotionally Before Leading Practically 7
   Building Trust and Loyalty 11
3 Chapter 3: The Law of Respect 15
   Earning Respect to Gain Followers 15
   Principles to Strengthen Your Leadership Presence 19

II Part 2: Empowering Others through Leadership

4 Chapter 4: The Law of Empowerment 25
   Leading by Letting Go 25
   Creating an Environment for Growth 29
5 Chapter 5: The Law of Addition 34
   Leadership Adds Value by Serving Others 34
   Strategies for Building Up Those You Lead 37
6 Chapter 6: The Law of Magnetism 42
   Who You Are Is Who You Attract 42
   How Personal Growth Magnifies Leadership 46

III Part 3: Achieving Results through Leadership

7 Chapter 7: The Law of Navigation	53
Charting a Clear Path Forward	53
Guiding Others through Challenges	57
8 Chapter 8: The Law of Victory	61
Leaders Find a Way to Win	61
The Unwavering Mindset of Success	65
9 Chapter 9: The Law of the Big Picture	69
Seeing Beyond the Immediate	69
Aligning Vision, Strategy, and Execution	73

IV Part 4: Building Lasting Influence and Legacy

10 Chapter 10: The Law of Timing	79
Understanding When to Act	79
Balancing Patience and Urgency	83
11 Chapter 11: The Law of Legacy	87
Leadership's Greatest Reward: Leaving a Legacy	87
Building a Sustainable Culture of Leadership	91
12 Chapter 12: The Law of Reproduction	96
Leaders Develop Leaders	96
Strategies to Multiply Your Impact	99

V Part 5: Mastering Leadership through Reflection and Practice

13 Chapter 13: The Law of Consistency	107
Stability Breeds Trust	107
Practicing What You Preach	110
14 Chapter 14: The Law of Priorities	114
Knowing What Must Come First	114
How to Focus on What Matters Most	118

15	Chapter 15: The Law of Sacrifice	122
	Great Leadership Requires Giving Up to Go Up	122
	Learning When and How to Sacrifice	125
16	Chapter 16: The Law of Intuition	129
	Leaders Read Situations and People	129
	Developing an Insightful Leadership Approach	132
17	Chapter 17: The Law of Momentum	136
	The Power of Positive Momentum in Leadership	136
	How to Start and Sustain Momentum in a Team	139
18	Chapter 18: The Law of Buy-In	143
	Gaining Commitment and Ownership	143
	Earning People's Trust and Support	146
19	Chapter 19: The Law of the Inner Circle	150
	Leaders' Strength Is Their Inner Circle	150
	Building a Team of Trusted Advisors	153
20	Chapter 20: The Law of Influence Multiplication	157
	Multiplying Influence through Collaboration	157
	Maximizing Impact by Leading with Others	160
21	Chapter 21: The Law of Legacy Building	164
	Crafting a Lasting Influence	164
	Action Step:	167
	Building Systems and Succession Planning	167
22	Conclusion	171

Introduction

Leadership is more than just a position or a title it's a choice. A choice to influence, inspire, and create change. Yet, for many, the question remains: What does it take to truly lead? In a world where authority can be granted but leadership must be earned, the journey to becoming a leader is not merely about power, but about impact.

The laws of leadership presented in this book are not theories or abstract ideas they are timeless principles that have shaped the success of the world's greatest leaders. Whether you are leading a company, a team, a community, or even just yourself, these laws are the blueprint for achieving lasting influence and significance.

Why These 21 Laws Matter

You might be wondering, why 21 laws? Why not just one guiding principle, or a simple checklist of do's and don'ts? The reality is that leadership is multifaceted. Each law addresses a distinct, crucial aspect of what it means to be an effective leader. They cover the nuances of connecting with others, navigating challenges, and making decisions that leave a lasting legacy. They are not about shortcuts but enduring truths, applicable regardless of your background, role, or industry.

Some may view leadership as an exclusive club a privilege reserved for a chosen few. But I believe that leadership is a journey, not a destination, and it's one that anyone can undertake. You don't need to be born with a specific set of skills or qualities. You just need the willingness to learn, to grow, and to serve others. And that's exactly what this book aims to help you achieve.

How to Use This Book to Transform Your Leadership

This book is structured to guide you through each of the 21 laws in a clear and practical way. Each chapter will introduce you to a specific law, explain why it matters, and provide real-life examples of how it has been applied by influential leaders throughout history. You'll read about leaders who have achieved remarkable success not because they were born exceptional, but because they committed themselves to learning and embodying these laws.

Along the way, you will find actionable steps that allow you to reflect on and apply each principle to your own life. Leadership is a practice, and these laws are designed to be lived, not just read. As you immerse yourself in this journey, I encourage you to pause at the end of each chapter, take a moment to reflect, and ask yourself how you can implement that law in your personal and professional life.

The Challenge and the Opportunity

Leadership is not easy. It demands self-discipline, sacrifice, and courage. It asks you to put others first, to make hard decisions, and to continuously strive for growth. But it's also one of the most fulfilling paths you can choose. As a leader, you have the power to inspire others, to create positive change, and to leave a legacy that outlasts you.

This book is an invitation. An invitation to step up and lead with authenticity, integrity, and purpose. To challenge yourself, to embrace the discomfort of growth, and to commit to a higher standard of leadership. Because in a world where so many follow, we need leaders who are willing to pave the way.

So, if you're ready to take on that challenge, let's begin this journey together. Remember, leadership is not about what you do it's about who you become. And through these 21 laws, you have the opportunity to become the leader you were meant to be.

I

Part 1: The Foundation of Leadership

1

Chapter 1: The Law of Influence

Leadership Defined by Influence, Not Title

"The key to successful leadership today is influence, not authority."
— Ken Blanchard

We frequently associate leadership with titles, jobs, or job descriptions. In organizations and communities, persons at the top of the hierarchy are considered leaders. However, true leadership is more than just the nameplate on your office door; it is about the impact you make, the trust you foster, and the influence you have over people. Leadership is about acquiring influence rather than having authority.

What is influence, and why is it important?

Influence is the ability to influence the behavior, development, or decisions of others. When you truly lead, you inspire others to think, act, and grow in a positive and meaningful way. This influence is not based on your position of authority or the size of your salary. It arises from your capacity to connect with others, establish trust, and motivate others to pursue your goal.

Consider this: How often do we see people in positions of leadership struggling to motivate and guide those around them? They have the title but lack influence. On the other side, innumerable people with no formal title or authority encourage others to follow their example solely through their acts, character, and words. This is because leadership is a choice rather than an appointment. And that choice is based on one's power to influence.

Misconception of Leadership Titles

Consider titles like caps that we wear. They can be altered, removed, or moved. What about influence? That reflects who we are. It symbolizes genuineness, respect, and credibility. Titles may provide you with power for a time, but only influence allows you to continually lead others.

When people follow you because of your title, their dedication is often insufficient. They may cooperate out of necessity or fear of repercussions, but their loyalty is fleeting. True leadership, however, builds a deeper connection. It fosters a following via respect and a shared belief in a common goal. People who follow you because of your influence have true devotion and long-term loyalty.

How to Build Influence as a Leader

1. Build Trust Through Authenticity

- People are drawn to leaders who are authentic and open. Being authentic does not imply oversharing or attempting to be everyone's best friend; it entails adhering to your ideals and acting with integrity. When your words match your actions, you establish trust the cornerstone of power.

2. Connect Before You Lead

- To influence people, you must connect with them on a human level. Demonstrate empathy by actively listening and taking the time to comprehend their points of view. Great leaders do not only speak; they listen and make others feel heard.

3. Demonstrate Competence and Consistency

- Influence rises when others believe in your ability and trust you. Showcase your competence through your actions, decisions, and outcomes. Consistency is essential when you regularly make sensible decisions and treat others properly, you gain credibility, which develops influence.

4. Lead with Humility and Purpose

- People do not support those who pursue power for its own sake. They follow leaders who believe in a higher cause and are dedicated to helping others. Humility isn't about being meek or downplaying your accomplishments; it's about realizing that leadership isn't about you, but about empowering others to do their best.

Ripple Effect of Influence

When you lead by influence, you generate a ripple effect that spreads beyond yourself. Your words and deeds inspire others, who then impact those around them. Influence, unlike authority, does not remain contained within a hierarchy; it expands organically, reinforcing the culture and encouraging collective growth.

Consider the story of Nelson Mandela. Mandela's influence was defined not by his position as President of South Africa, but by his persistent commitment to peace and justice. He made profound connections with individuals, earning their trust through authenticity, empathy, and sacrifice. His impact went far beyond his political position, encouraging millions around the world to fight for equality and peace. Mandela proved that influence-based leadership leaves an enduring legacy.

Reflection: Do You Rely on Titles or Build Influence?

As you embark on your leadership journey, pause and ask yourself: Are you relying on your title or earning influence? Do people follow you because of your position, or because they believe and respect you? Leadership defined by influence necessitates persistent effort, real concern for others, and a willingness to serve.

Action Step:

Identify one area where you can increase your influence. It might be making stronger connections with your team, being more transparent in your decisions, or simply being more consistent in your behavior. Consider how you might win trust and respect based on your character and expertise rather than authority.

2

Chapter 2: The Law of Connection

Connecting Emotionally Before Leading Practically

"People don't care how much you know until they know how much you care." — John C. Maxwell

When we think about leadership, strategy, and decision-making frequently spring to mind first. However, effective leadership is more than just delivering orders or creating goals; it is also about connecting with those you lead. Leadership is a relational endeavor, and those who master the art of connecting build the most resilient, devoted teams.

According to the Law of Connection, leaders must first touch someone's heart before asking for their hand. In other words, before you can effectively lead others, you must first establish an emotional connection with them. Only then will you be able to influence and direct them practically.

Why Does Emotional Connection Matter in Leadership?

Every strong leader can profoundly connect with people. Emotional connections promote trust, loyalty, and a sense of belonging. It bridges the gap between intentions and deeds, changing a transactional relationship into something meaningful. When leaders engage emotionally, they communicate with empathy and understanding rather than just words.

Consider a manager who leads their staff without ever engaging in actual talks, addressing their concerns, or expressing gratitude. Even if their instructions are clear, something important is missing: trust and rapport. Compare this to a leader who knows the names of each team member's children, actively listens throughout meetings, and celebrates both major and minor successes. Which leader would you follow more willingly?

The Difference Between Compliance and Commitment.

Connecting emotionally lays the groundwork for trust, which is the cornerstone of commitment. When you connect with others, you acquire more than just their cooperation; you gain their trust and dedication. They aren't just following your directions; they're aligning themselves with your vision. Without this emotional connection, leaders may discover that they are receiving little effort or that their staff is disinterested.

The capacity to connect enables leaders to progress beyond superficial conformity to genuine commitment, in which others believe in the leader's vision and purpose. Emotional connection drives people to go the additional mile, provide unique ideas, and remain devoted even in difficult circumstances.

How to Connect with People Emotionally

1. Listen Actively and Attentively

- Connection starts with listening. People want to feel heard and understood. Listening is more than just nodding along or waiting your turn to speak. It entails giving your complete attention, acknowledging what is said, and reacting wisely. When you actively listen to others, you demonstrate that their opinions and concerns are important, which deepens your relationship with them.

CHAPTER 2: THE LAW OF CONNECTION

2. Show Empathy and Compassion.

- Empathy is the ability to put oneself in someone else's shoes and see things through their eyes. Empathetic leaders comprehend their team members' issues, feelings, and experiences. Empathy makes leadership more relatable and approachable. Compassionate leaders don't just acknowledge difficulties; they also provide support, guidance, and encouragement.

3. Be Authentic and Vulnerable

- Authenticity fosters connection. When you are honest about your challenges, setbacks, and even anxieties, you become more relatable. Leaders who pretend to be perfect frequently build obstacles rather than bridges. Being authentic does not imply oversharing every detail; rather, it entails being honest about what you know and don't know, as well as demonstrating that you are also human.

4. Express Genuine Appreciation

- People seek acknowledgment and gratitude for their work. A simple "thank you" or sincere recognition of hard effort can go a long way toward establishing an emotional attachment. Leaders who regularly express thanks foster an environment of appreciation and mutual respect.

5. Communicate Clearly and Often

- Clear and consistent communication helps people connect with the organization's vision and mission. But it's more than just providing information; it's also about fostering an open discussion in which input is encouraged and appreciated. Leaders who speak openly promote transparency, which strengthens trust.

The Ripple Effect of Emotional Connection

When leaders connect emotionally, they foster an environment in which employees feel seen, heard, and valued. This connection has a knock-on effect, affecting not only individual relationships but also the dynamics of the entire organization. Teams led by emotionally linked leaders are more likely to be engaged, cohesive, and driven.

Consider the story of Howard Schultz, CEO of Starbucks. Schultz created more than simply a business; he also established a culture. He dedicated time and effort to interact with them on a personal level, knowing their names and stories. Schultz's emotional connection to his employees resulted in a company culture in which everyone felt appreciated and a part of something larger than themselves. This technique helped Starbucks become one of the world's most well-known and successful companies.

Reflection: Are you leading or managing?

Leading without connecting is simply managing. Managers manage employees to fulfill tasks, whereas leaders connect with them and motivate them to achieve a common goal. Ask yourself: Are you just concerned with getting things done, or are you also interested in developing meaningful relationships with those you lead?

Action Step:

This week, make a conscious effort to connect emotionally with a member of your team. It could be by taking a few extra minutes to listen, showing gratitude, or just enquiring about their difficulties and providing assistance. Remember that little deeds can have a huge impact on relationships.

Building Trust and Loyalty

"Trust is the glue of life. It's the most essential ingredient in effective communication. It's the foundational principle that holds all relationships." — Stephen Covey

Leadership does not develop overnight, and it cannot be sustained solely by authority. Every successful leader has the capacity to build trust. Trust is what elevates leadership from a position of power to one of influence. It's what keeps relationships alive, creates loyalty, and allows individuals to collaborate toward a common objective. Trust is the foundation upon which all effective leadership is founded.

According to the Law of Trust, loyalty can only be won after trust has been built. Even the most skilled leaders will struggle to convince people to follow them if they lack trust. After all, leadership is about convincing people to believe in who you are and where you're headed, not just doing what you say.

Why trust is more important than ever

In today's fast-paced and constantly changing world, trust is more important than ever. People are less trusting of authority and more selective about who they follow. They want leaders that are not only talented, but also sincere, consistent, and have their best interests in mind. When people trust you, they give you more than simply their collaboration; they give you their loyalty and dedication.

But faith cannot be demanded or imposed. It must be earned, developed, and reinforced by your actions and choices. It's a frail but powerful link that, once destroyed, is nearly impossible to repair. Leaders who understand this and prioritize trust in their relationships will automatically attract loyal and passionate followers.

How to Build Trust as a Leader

1. Lead with Integrity and Authenticity

- Integrity is the foundation of trust. Integrity implies consistently operating by your ideals and principles, even if it is uncomfortable or controversial. Authenticity means being genuine to yourself rather than attempting to be someone you are not. When people perceive that you are honest and unwavering in your integrity, they feel comfortable placing their trust in you.

2. Communicate Openly and Transparently

- Leaders who speak honestly build trust more quickly than those who keep people in the dark. Transparency is being open about obstacles, admitting mistakes, and communicating your ideas and judgments. People want to be involved in the trip, not merely directed to the end. When you keep people informed, you foster a culture of trust in which everyone feels valued and appreciated.

3. Deliver on Your Promises

- Trust is created one commitment at a time. People need to know that you will keep your promises, no matter how big or small. Every promise honored builds trust, but every promise violated weakens it. Make thoughtful promises, and then give them your all.

4. Show Empathy and Care

- Leaders who demonstrate empathy earn the trust of the people they lead. Empathy is the ability to comprehend and share the emotions of another person. It's more than just acknowledging difficulties; it's about actually caring about the well-being of those you supervise. When others believe you genuinely care, they confide in you with their vulnerabilities and challenges.

5. Take Responsibility and Be Accountable

- Nobody expects a leader to be perfect, but they do expect a leader to be responsible. When you make mistakes, confess it. When you fall short, admit it. Accountability demonstrates your willingness to learn and improve, which fosters trust over time. Avoid transferring responsibility or making excuses, as these behaviors swiftly undermine trust.

The Relationship Between Trust and Loyalty

Trust naturally leads to loyalty. When people trust you, they become more than just followers; they are advocates. They believe in you and your cause, and they are willing to support you even when the going gets tough. Loyal followers do not simply follow blindly; they actively support and contribute to your vision because they trust the person leading them.

However, remember that loyalty is not the same as mindless allegiance. It's based on mutual respect and shared beliefs. As a leader, if you break trust or act inconsistently with your ideals, loyalty will swiftly diminish. Loyal followers want leaders to keep their word and to act by their principles.

The Power of Trust in Times of Crisis

Trust is especially crucial during times of distress. When uncertainty and challenges arise, people turn to leaders they can trust. During such moments, trust acts as a stabilizing force, enabling teams to traverse turbulence with resilience and togetherness. Leaders who have established trust before a crisis find it simpler to remain calm, guide effectively, and unite their staff to fight adversity.

Consider the leadership of Jacinda Ardern, New Zealand's former prime minister. During emergencies such as the Christchurch terror incident and the COVID-19 pandemic, Ardern's persistent communication, empathy, and decisive responses gained her citizens' trust and loyalty. Her leadership embodied the Law of Trust, demonstrating that when people believe in you, they will follow you through the most difficult situations.

Reflection: Are you trustworthy?

Ask yourself: Are you leading in a way that builds trust and loyalty? Do others believe your words, actions, and intentions? Building trust requires an ongoing commitment to living with honesty, authenticity, and responsibility.

Action Step:

This week, assess your pledges and responsibilities to others. Determine one area in which you can be more honest, provide more consistently, or demonstrate more empathy. Remember that trust is not established through spectacular gestures but by everyday deeds.

3

Chapter 3: The Law of Respect

Earning Respect to Gain Followers

"The very essence of leadership is that you have to have a vision. It's got to be a vision you articulate clearly and forcefully on every occasion. You can't blow an uncertain trumpet." — Reverend Theodore M. Hesburgh

To lead others, you must first gain their respect. Leadership is not bestowed by position or title; it is earned through continuous actions and steadfast values. People instinctively follow leaders they respect, and respect is earned over time via demonstrated skill, honesty, and devotion.

The Law of Respect states that people will follow leaders who have gained their admiration and confidence. Respect is not given freely; it must be earned by displaying qualities that inspire and drive people to willingly follow your example.

What Respect Means in Leadership

Respect in leadership is more than adoration or liking; it means being recognized for your character, ability, and actions. People who appreciate you believe in your decisions, agree with your vision and trust your judgment. Respect is not required; it is inspired by your example, how you handle obstacles, and how you treat others around you.

Leadership is frequently challenged in how you deal with adversity, the values you uphold, and the fairness you exhibit. Respect reflects your honesty, consistency, and boldness. When you earn the respect of others, you gain the capacity to favorably influence and confidently lead others.

The Difference Between Authority and Respect

Having authority does not ensure respect. In truth, people frequently obey authority but freely follow respect. Authority comes from a position, however respect comes from your deeds and personality. A leader who possesses power but lacks respect would struggle to generate loyalty and excitement. A leader who has won respect, even without formal authority, has significantly greater influence over others.

Respect turns compliance become a commitment. When people respect you, they go beyond their commitments and commit to your vision and objective. They put their energy, ingenuity, and passion into supporting you because they believe in you.

How to Earn Respect as a Leader

1. Demonstrate Competence and Expertise

- People admire leaders who are informed and skilled in their industry. When you demonstrate mastery over your responsibilities, make wise decisions, and successfully handle challenges, you earn the respect of others around you. Competence inspires confidence, which develops respect.

2. Show Consistency and Integrity

- Leaders who win respect demonstrate consistency in their principles and conduct. Integrity entails doing what is right, even if it is difficult or controversial. When you lead with integrity, people notice that your words match your actions, and they believe you will uphold your principles even under pressure.

3. Embody Courage and Stand Firm in Your Beliefs

- People admire leaders who stick to their convictions and principles, particularly in the face of hardship. Courageous leaders earn respect by taking chances, making difficult decisions, and speaking up when it counts the most. Courage does not imply fearlessness; rather, it is pressing forward despite your fears because you trust in the bigger goal.

4. Treat Others with Fairness and Respect

- Respect is reciprocal. If you want to be respected, first respect others. Respected leaders are known for their fairness; they treat everyone with dignity, listen objectively, and cherish everyone's contributions. When others feel appreciated, they are more likely to respect you.

5. Be Humble and Willing to Learn

- Great leaders establish respect not by claiming to know everything, but by demonstrating an eagerness to learn from others. Humility is not about humbling oneself; it is about acknowledging that you do not have all of the answers and appreciating the contributions of those you lead. When you recognize your faults, recognize others' strengths, and seek their opinions, you display the humility that earns respect.

The Impact of Earning Respect

When you win respect, you foster a culture of trust and commitment. People become more receptive to your instruction and willing to align with your ideas. Leaders who have earned respect can motivate others to go above and beyond because their followers have shown true devotion.

Consider the leadership of Martin Luther King Jr. Despite overcoming enormous hurdles, King gained respect for his unrelenting commitment to nonviolence, equality, and justice. He remained steadfast in his ideas and led by example, motivating millions to support his cause. King commanded not only authority but also national esteem, and his legacy continues to inspire people all across the world.

Reflection: Are You Earning or Expecting Respect?

Respect cannot be commanded; it must be earned through constant effort and deliberate action. Ask yourself: Are you leading in a way that earns respect, or are you expecting respect because of your position? Respect stems from expertise, honesty, and courage, therefore consider whether your activities reflect these qualities.

Action Step:

Identify an area for improvement in exhibiting competence, honesty, or fairness. Take a little, deliberate step this week to embody that progress. Remember that respect is not acquired by great gestures, but through persistent, everyday behaviors that reflect your ideals.

CHAPTER 3: THE LAW OF RESPECT

Principles to Strengthen Your Leadership Presence

"Leadership is not about being in charge. It's about taking care of those in your charge." — Simon Sinek

Leadership is more than just what you say or do; it is also about how you affect people simply by being present. Leadership presence is a set of attributes and behaviours that instill confidence, establish trust, and force people to follow. Great leaders have a presence that draws people in, commands respect, and instills a feeling of stability and direction.

According to the Law of Presence, leadership presence is achieved by embodying ideals that instill confidence, inspire others, and foster a sense of authenticity. It's the invisible yet indisputable energy that allows you to favorably affect others simply by being present in the room.

Why Leadership Presence Matters

Leadership presence is what distinguishes influential leaders from the rest. It is the distinction between leaders who simply give orders and those who inspire action with their demeanor, confidence, and composure. A leader with a presence does not need to demand authority; their confidence, poise, and genuineness establish their impact.

Leadership presence makes a strong first impression, but it extends beyond appearances. It refers to how you constantly hold yourself, speak, and interact with others. Leaders who radiate presence are those who remain cool in crisis, listen intently, and inspire trust through genuineness.

Principles for Strengthening Your Leadership Presence

1. Cultivate Self-Confidence Without Arrogance

- Confidence is the foundation of leadership presence, yet there is a thin line between it and arrogance. True confidence stems from understanding

your talents and being comfortable with who you are. It's not about claiming superiority; it's about believing in yourself and expressing that belief through your words and actions.
- Arrogance, on the other hand, is rooted in insecurity and frequently emerges as a need to prove oneself or denigrate others. To improve your leadership presence, cultivate confidence based on competence and self-awareness, rather than superiority.

2. Practice Mindful Communication

- Your communication style has a significant impact on your overall presence. Leaders with a presence speak effectively, listen intently, and demonstrate empathy. Mindful communication entails being fully present in interactions and paying attention to both what is said and how it is delivered. Leaders who actively listen foster a sense of value and respect, which strengthens their influence and trustworthiness.
- Pay attention to your tone, body language, and the emotions of the people you're speaking with. Effective leaders do more than simply transmit information; they engage on a deeper level by demonstrating comprehension and genuine interest.

3. Embody Authenticity and Integrity

- Authentic leaders do not wear disguises or pretend to be someone they are not. Authenticity refers to being genuine and consistent in your values, words, and actions. When you're authentic, people can tell—they know you're being honest with them, which builds trust.
- Integrity is an extension of sincerity in decision-making and behavior. It implies doing the right thing, even if it is unpleasant or uncomfortable. Leaders who lead with integrity have a stronger presence because their actions are consistent with their ideals.

4. Maintain Composure Under Pressure

- Leadership presence is most noticeable in difficult times. When pressure mounts and emotions run high, leaders with presence remain calm, collected, and focused. This calmness portrays stability and strength, calming people and allowing them to stay focused in the face of uncertainty.
- Maintaining composure does not imply concealing emotions or ignoring challenges. It entails acknowledging the obstacles and deciding to respond carefully rather than hastily. Composure under pressure necessitates self-awareness, emotional management, and a strong sense of purpose.

5. Demonstrate Empathy and Compassion

- Leadership is more than just directing others; it is about understanding and caring for them. Leaders with presence express empathy by recognizing their followers' struggles, concerns, and desires. Compassionate leaders foster a safe environment in which individuals feel seen, listened to, and supported.
- Empathy does not weaken a leader; rather, it makes them more relatable and approachable. By demonstrating genuine concern for others, you increase trust and enhance your connection with those you lead, so strengthening your presence.

6. Show Consistency in Actions and Values

- Consistency is essential for developing credibility and strengthening your leadership presence. When you continuously display your values and act with integrity, people begin to trust your character. Inconsistency, on the other side, undermines trust and reduces your visibility as a leader.
- Strive to be the same person in every situation, regardless of the pressures you are under. Consistency does not imply inflexibility; it is sticking to your ideals and values even when circumstances change.

The Ripple Effect of Strong Leadership Presence

A strong leadership presence has a contagious influence on teams and organizations. When people are around a confident, authentic, and empathic leader, they feel inspired, comfortable, and motivated. Leadership presence establishes the tone, shapes the atmosphere, and influences how people feel and behave.

Consider the case of Nelson Mandela. Mandela's presence was apparent; he was inspired not only with words, but also with his unwavering ideals, sensitivity, and ability to remain calm in the face of hardship. His presence was not about authority; rather, it was about embodying traits that inspired people to believe in themselves and their larger mission.

Reflection: Are You Strengthening Your Presence or Focusing Solely on Actions?

Ask yourself: Are you focussing on doing more as a leader, or are you striving to become a leader whose presence inspires trust and confidence? Actions are crucial, but leadership presence includes how you show up, how you interact with others, and how you inspire confidence via sincerity and calmness.

Action Step:

This week, choose one principle to improve your leadership presence. Whether it's practicing attentive communication, displaying empathy, or developing self-confidence, make an effort to exemplify this value in your interactions. Remember that leadership presence is not about making great gestures; it is about continually embodying attributes that engender trust and influence.

II

Part 2: Empowering Others through Leadership

4

Chapter 4: The Law of Empowerment

Leading by Letting Go

"**T**he greatest leader is not necessarily the one who does the greatest things. He is the one that gets the people to do the greatest things.**"** — Ronald Reagan

One of the most difficult but essential talents for any leader is the capacity to let go. Leaders have a natural need to maintain control they want to oversee every decision, ensure every outcome, and personally drive every process. True leadership, however, is about knowing when to let go and empowering others to take the lead.

The Law of Empowerment states that a leader's influence and impact grow not by doing everything themselves, but by empowering and trusting others to take responsibility. It takes humility to step back and boldness to allow others to walk forward.

The paradox of control in leadership

At first appearance, the concept of letting go appears paradoxical to leadership. Isn't a leader supposed to guide, direct, and ensure things proceed as planned? Yes, but holding on too tightly can create bottlenecks, hinder creativity, and impede growth both for you as a leader and for those you lead.

Great leaders recognize that their role is not to accomplish everything alone, but to provide an environment in which others can do their best. Leadership is fundamentally about unleashing potential rather than exerting control.

Why letting go is essential for leadership.

1. Empowerment promotes trust and confidence

- When you empower others, you are not only giving them responsibility; you are also demonstrating that you trust them. Trust is the foundation of all successful teams. When people feel trusted, they gain confidence in their talents, become more engaged in their work, and are more invested in the organization's success.

2. Letting go promotes innovation and growth

- Leaders who attempt to control everything may unintentionally limit innovation. By letting go, you make room for fresh ideas, different perspectives, and creative solutions. Empowered team members are allowed to think outside the box and take initiative, which promotes personal development and organizational success.

3. Delegation increases your leadership capacity

- There's just so much you can accomplish on your own. Leaders who delegate effectively increase their potential by drawing on the talents and skills of others. This allows you to focus on strategic decisions and high-impact areas while delegating specifics to your team.

How to Lead by letting go

1. Delegate with Intention

- Letting go does not imply abandoning your obligations; rather, it entails delegating purposefully and intelligently. Identify tasks and decisions that others can handle, then delegate them with clear expectations and guidelines. When you delegate with intention, you demonstrate that you value other people's contributions and believe in their talents.

2. Provide guidance, not micromanagement

- Letting go does not imply complete withdrawal; rather, it involves transitioning from micromanaging to assisting. Provide direction, mentorship, and feedback without hovering or second-guessing each action. When people know you're there to help them, not manage them, they feel more confident and willing to take responsibility.

3. Encourage autonomy and accountability

- Empowerment is more than just assigning jobs; it is about providing people the autonomy to make decisions and the accountability to own the outcomes. Encourage team members to take the initiative and trust their judgment. When people are given both the freedom to act and the responsibility to deliver, they increase their competence and confidence.

4. Embrace the possibility of mistakes

- Letting go entails admitting that mistakes will occur. However, mistakes are not failures; rather, they provide possibilities for progress. Leaders who empower people must be willing to tolerate occasional mistakes as part of the learning process. Instead of blaming people, provide instruction and support to help them grow and improve.

5. Recognize and Celebrate Contributions

- Empowerment is incomplete without acknowledgment. Recognize the contributions, efforts, and accomplishments of those you lead. When employees feel rewarded for their efforts, they become more driven and devoted. Celebrate both minor accomplishments and significant milestones, and let your team know that their efforts are appreciated.

Benefits of Empowerment in Leadership

Empowering people does not lessen your impact; rather, it increases it. When people are given the opportunity and support to lead in their areas of expertise, their collective impact grows. Leaders who empower others foster a culture of collaboration, trust, and ongoing development. They inspire loyalty, stimulate innovation, and leave a legacy that extends beyond their accomplishments.

Consider the leadership of Mahatma Gandhi. Gandhi's influence sprang not from authority or control, but from his ability to inspire millions to take ownership of their own freedom and dignity. He encouraged an entire nation to rise and make change by relying on others to contribute to the cause and adopting a nonviolent resistance mindset.

Reflection: Are You Empowered or Controlling?

Consider whether you are leading by empowering people or holding on too tightly to maintain control. Empowerment necessitates humility and courage. It entails accepting that your responsibility is not to do everything, but rather to unlock the potential in others around you.

Action Step:

This week, select one area in which you may let go and delegate responsibilities to another person. Communicate your trust, provide the appropriate assistance, and allow them to make their own decisions. Observe the results and be ready to provide advice, not micromanagement.

Creating an Environment for Growth

"The function of leadership is to produce more leaders, not more followers."
— Ralph Nader

Effective leaders recognize that progress does not occur in isolation it thrives in the appropriate context. People, like seeds, require an atmosphere that supports and stimulates their growth. The Law of the Environment emphasizes the leader's role in creating an environment in which individuals and teams can thrive, develop, and realize their greatest potential.

The environment you create as a leader influences the behavior, mindset, and goals of those around you. Your impact goes beyond what you accomplish; it permeates the environment you create and the ideals you defend. Leaders who foster a growth mindset inspire others to take risks, strive for greatness, and always improve.

Impact of the Right Environment

Imagine a workplace where employees feel respected, supported, and encouraged to advance. Individuals in such an environment are more motivated, interested, and willing to learn. They see obstacles as opportunities, collaborate freely, and are proud of their efforts. In contrast, in a suffocating workplace characterized by fear, micromanagement, or rigid hierarchies, individuals become disengaged, risk-averse, and resistant to change.

Great leaders understand that they have the ability to affect their surroundings and foster an environment that encourages growth. The atmosphere you create has a direct impact on not only individual development, but also team cohesion, innovation, and overall performance.

Principles of Creating an Environment for Growth

1. Foster a culture of trust and psychological safety

- Growth cannot exist in the absence of trust. People who feel psychologically comfortable are more willing to share their opinions, voice their worries, and take risks. Leaders who develop trust create an environment in which people feel valued, supported, and free to be themselves.
- Build trust by communicating frankly, admitting mistakes, and listening without judgment. Make it clear that mistakes are part of the learning process, not a reason for punishment. When people feel safe being vulnerable, they are more likely to push themselves beyond their comfort zones.

2. Encourage continuous learning and curiosity

- Growth-oriented environments encourage a culture of learning and inquiry. Encourage your team to seek out fresh information, experiment with novel ideas, and question traditional wisdom. Leaders who embrace learning show a willingness to grow themselves and illustrate that progress is a lifelong process.
- Create opportunities for professional development, offer skill-building materials, and recognize people who value learning. When people sense that progress is encouraged and supported, they are more likely to seek out new possibilities and broaden their skills.

3. Embrace diversity and inclusion

- A growth-oriented atmosphere must welcome and celebrate varied views

and perspectives. Accepting diversity of thinking, experience, and background improves problem-solving, ignites creativity, and promotes innovation.
- Inclusive leaders aggressively seek and value diverse viewpoints. They understand that diversity is more than just a checkbox it is a source of strength and a driver of growth. Create an inclusive workplace by actively listening, addressing biases, and providing space for all views to be heard.

4. Set high standards and offer constructive feedback

- Leaders who foster growth establish high-performance standards while providing the necessary assistance to achieve them. High standards motivate people to rise beyond mediocrity, whereas constructive feedback provides the assistance required to progress.
- However, setting high standards does not imply being excessively critical or demanding perfection. It entails trusting in the capabilities of those you lead and keeping them accountable to strive for excellence. When you set clear expectations and give constructive comments, you enable others to grow in an organized and supportive manner.

5. Celebrate progress and recognize achievements

- Growth necessitates recognition and celebration. When people's efforts and achievements are acknowledged, they are driven to keep progressing. Leaders who foster growth make it a habit to applaud not only the result but also the steps taken toward it.
- Take the time to recognize milestones and little victories. Recognise individual and team accomplishments, and express sincere gratitude for the work made. Celebrating progress increases momentum, reinforces a growth mentality, and fosters a sense of purpose and pride in your team.

6. Empower ownership and accountability

- Growth thrives in an environment where employees have a sense of ownership over their jobs. When people have autonomy and are held accountable for their contributions, they become more committed to their development and the success of the team.
- Empower your team members to accept responsibility for their initiatives and decisions. Give them the authority to lead in their areas of responsibility, and hold them accountable for the results. Ownership instills a sense of pride and responsibility, which promotes personal and professional development.

The Role of Leadership in Fostering Growth

Leadership is more than just directing work and managing outcomes; it is also about encouraging the development of others. Leaders who prioritize fostering a growth-oriented atmosphere understand that their success is evaluated not by their accomplishments, but by the development and empowerment of those they supervise.

Consider the leadership of Warren Buffett, a well-known businessman and philanthropist. Throughout his career, Buffett has emphasized the necessity of establishing an environment in which talented individuals may take responsibility and thrive. His belief in the potential of others, as well as his dedication to developing trust and autonomy, have enabled his team and businesses to grow and succeed.

Reflection: Is your environment conducive to growth?

Consider whether the environment you're creating promotes growth or stifles the potential of those around you. Growth necessitates a deliberate emphasis on trust, inclusion, learning, and accountability.

Action Step:

This week, pinpoint one area of your surroundings that may be impeding progress and take a tiny, deliberate step to fix it. Make a concerted effort to create a more growth-oriented workplace, whether it's by building trust, embracing diversity, or establishing clearer standards.

5

Chapter 5: The Law of Addition

Leadership Adds Value by Serving Others

"The highest of distinctions is service to others." — King George VI

Leadership is fundamentally about service, not power or glory. Leadership is really about having a good impact on the lives of people. According to the Law of Addition, leaders elevate others by serving them selflessly and putting their well-being, progress, and success first.

Great leaders recognize that their influence is measured not by their authority, but by the value they add. The greatest enduring legacies are based not on titles or accomplishments, but on the lives they have touched and the contributions they have made to other people's successes.

The Shift from Being Self-Serving to Being Service-Minded

It's tempting to conceive of leadership as being in charge or accomplishing tasks. However, leaders who are completely focused on their agenda frequently fail to gain the trust and allegiance of the people they serve. Leaders who approach their roles with a service perspective, on the other hand, build stronger bonds, inspire true devotion, and leave a lasting impression.

The transition from self-serving to service-minded begins with a basic adjustment in perspective: it's no longer about what you can have, but what you can offer. The most influential leaders see themselves not as the pinnacle of a hierarchy, but as the base from which others might climb.

Principles of Adding Value Through Service

1. Prioritize the needs of others

- Adding value begins with understanding the needs of those you lead. It takes active listening, empathy, and a willingness to prioritize the interests of others over your own. Leaders who serve prioritize learning what their team members require to succeed and then taking action to address those requirements.
- To add value, endeavor to understand your team's difficulties, motivations, and goals. By doing so, you demonstrate that you care about their development and well-being.

2. Invest in the development of your team

- Leaders who serve are dedicated to the growth and development of their teams. They understand that their legacy is determined not by their accomplishments, but by the people they help elevate. Investing in the development of others entails offering mentorship, encouragement, and chances for learning and growth.
- Consider how you may encourage people to take on new challenges, broaden their talents, and assume leadership roles of their own. Investing in people's development has a far-reaching impact.

3. Lead by Example with Humility and Service

- Leaders who offer value don't just talk about service; they live it. They set a good example by being humble, honest, and eager to help their

colleagues. This fosters mutual respect and establishes the foundation for a service-oriented culture.
- Humble leaders are approachable and responsive to feedback. They don't consider any duty beneath them, and they're eager to roll up their sleeves and help wherever they can. When you lead with humility, you gain trust and inspire others to follow suit.

4. Recognize and elevate the contributions of others

- True service-minded leadership does not take credit; rather, it recognizes and celebrates the efforts and accomplishments of others. Leaders who offer value inspire those they lead by acknowledging their efforts, celebrating their victories, and providing the credit they deserve.
- Recognize individual and team accomplishments and express sincere gratitude for efforts. When people feel appreciated for their work, they are encouraged to keep contributing value to others.

5. Empower others to become leaders

- Service-minded leaders seek to develop more leaders, not followers. They encourage others to take on leadership roles, share their expertise and experiences, and become agents of positive change. This strategy not only improves the team but also increases the effectiveness of service.
- Encourage your team members to take the initiative, coach others, and lead by example in their respective jobs. Empowering others to serve fosters a culture of collective leadership in which everyone is dedicated to making a difference.

The Legacy of a Service-Oriented Leader

Mother Teresa is a wonderful example of service-oriented leadership. Despite having no legal power, her unselfish dedication to aiding the poor and marginalized earned her the love and affection of millions of people around the world. Her leadership was characterized not by her position, but by the people she touched and the value she added through compassion and service.

Mother Teresa's history reminds us that the actual influence of leadership is not measured by titles or accolades but by the people we serve and the value we add. A service-minded leader leaves a legacy of transformed lives, empowered individuals, and a culture of selflessness that lasts beyond their term.

Reflection: Do You Add Value or Seek It?

Ask yourself: Are you actively adding value to those around you, or are you primarily concerned with your success? Intention and deeds distinguish a self-serving leader from a service-minded one. Service-minded leaders intentionally prioritize others and assess their success by the good influence they have.

Action Step:

This week, think about how you can help someone else by doing an act of service. Make a conscious effort to serve selflessly, whether by mentoring a team member, providing support to someone facing a hardship, or simply listening. Consider the impact it has on you and the people you serve.

Strategies for Building Up Those You Lead

"As we look ahead into the next century, leaders will be those who empower others." — Bill Gates

Great leaders do more than just accomplish personal achievement; they inspire and motivate those around them to fulfill their full potential. According to the Law of Empowerment, a leader's greatest strength is his or her ability to build up others under them. It's about building a culture in which people feel respected, supported, and prepared to give their all.

The ability to empower people is more than just a desirable trait; it is a defining characteristic of transformational leaders. Leaders who invest in empowering others build trust, encourage growth, and leave a legacy that goes beyond their accomplishments.

The Importance of Developing Those You Lead

Effective leadership is not about commanding from above; rather, it is about raising others from their current position. When you develop people you lead, you are not only improving their abilities; you are also increasing your own impact. A leader's success is strongly related to the performance of their team, and empowering others increases both individual and collective effect.

Empowerment generates feelings of ownership, motivation, and loyalty. It gives people the courage to take initiative and the ability to achieve in their jobs. Investing in those you lead develops a team of capable leaders who are ready to take on new challenges.

Strategies for Building Up Those You Lead

1. Give Trust and Autonomy

- Trust is the foundation of empowerment. Granting autonomy demonstrates trust by allowing people to take responsibility for their work and make decisions. Micromanagement stifles creativity and undermines confidence, whereas autonomy promotes invention and accountability.
- To empower others, find duties or obligations that can be delegated to others. Set clear expectations, then stand back and let them take the lead. Assist as needed, but avoid hovering. Show that you believe in their judgment, and they will rise to fulfill your expectations.

2. Mentor and coach with purpose

- Leaders who develop others do more than just direct; they also advise, mentor, and coach. Mentorship is the act of sharing your knowledge, experience, and wisdom with others in order to help them grow. It is about asking the correct questions, providing constructive feedback, and pushing others to go beyond their comfort zones.
- When mentoring or coaching, prioritize both professional and personal development. Assist individuals in identifying their talents, working through problems, and setting meaningful goals. Provide regular encouragement and serve as a sounding board for their ideas and goals.

3. Recognize and celebrate strengths

- When people feel valued for their abilities and accomplishments, they are more likely to develop and flourish. Building up others entails recognizing what they do well and expressing genuine gratitude for their efforts. Celebrating strengths not only builds confidence but also encourages people to keep growing.
- Take the time to recognize individual and team accomplishments, both publicly and individually. Celebrate not only results but also growth and effort. When people feel recognized for their skills, they are motivated to improve on them.

4. Create Opportunities for Leadership

- One of the most effective methods to develop those you lead is to provide them with leadership opportunities. This does not necessarily include providing formal titles; rather, it entails allowing individuals to lead projects, initiatives, and teams. Empowering people to lead promotes a sense of ownership, confidence, and the development of new talents.
- Identify areas where team members can take the initiative. Assist, but give them the freedom to make decisions and face obstacles on their own. Leadership opportunities help people broaden their horizons and reach their full potential.

5. Provide constructive feedback with care

- Constructive feedback is necessary for progress, but it must be given with care and intent. Leaders who empower people utilize feedback as a tool for progress rather than as a source of criticism. They approach feedback with empathy, emphasizing behavior and outcomes rather than personal characteristics.
- When providing feedback, begin by recognizing what the person did well before offering specific, practical suggestions for improvement. Frame your feedback as a chance for learning and growth, and convey your belief in their potential to make progress.

6. Encourage a Culture of Open Communication

- An empowered environment fosters open conversation. When people feel at ease sharing their opinions, asking questions, and expressing concerns, they are more likely to contribute their best ideas and work effectively. Leaders who encourage free communication foster an environment of trust and mutual respect.
- Foster an environment in which everyone's opinion is appreciated. Encourage others to share their thoughts, listen without passing judgment, and be receptive to feedback yourself. Open communication enhances relationships and promotes ongoing learning and progress.

The Ripple Effect of Empowerment

Building up the people you lead has a far-reaching impact on the organization as a whole. Empowered team members are more engaged, motivated, and devoted to the group objective. They motivate people to take the initiative, accept responsibility, and make important contributions.

Consider Mandela's leadership. Mandela's capacity to empower others was key to his influence. He did more than just lead a movement; he also taught people how to be leaders. Mandela enabled a nation to rise and shape its future by instilling a sense of togetherness, trust, and common purpose.

Reflection: Are you building or tearing down?

Ask yourself: Are you purposefully developing people you lead, or are you unintentionally holding them back? Empowerment necessitates a purposeful decision to trust, guide, and elevate others. It entails focussing not on your own strength, but on the potential of those you lead.

Action Step:

This week, choose one person to lead and take a particular action to empower them. Make a concerted effort to support their development, whether by encouraging them, delegating new responsibilities, or giving thoughtful coaching. Pay close attention to how this act of empowerment affects their confidence and contributions.

6

Chapter 6: The Law of Magnetism

Who You Are Is Who You Attract

"**Your actions and behavior, more than your words, will determine the people who follow you.**" — John C. Maxwell

Leadership is more than just what you do; it is about who you are. According to the Law of Magnetism, leaders attract those who share their values, attitudes, and perspectives. The traits and ideas you embody will influence the types of people who are drawn to you and eventually follow your lead.

Great leaders recognize that their inner world—their beliefs, character, and attitudes—determines their outside effect. If you want to attract and build a successful team, you must first become the type of leader who exemplifies the values you value in others. Your team becomes a reflection of your leadership.

Why Who You Are is Important in Leadership

People naturally gravitate towards leaders whom they respect, admire, and connect with. This relationship typically extends beyond skills and experience to common values, attitudes, and a sense of alignment with the leader's goal.

CHAPTER 6: THE LAW OF MAGNETISM

Who you are as an individual influences the culture, enthusiasm, and devotion of those you lead.

If you are driven, committed, and caring, you are likely to attract people who have those characteristics. However, if you lack integrity, suffer with discipline, or fail to communicate effectively, your team may reflect similar qualities. To attract and lead effectively, you must first focus on personal development.

Principles of the Law of Magnetism

1. Values Alignment

- Your values are the fundamental principles that govern your choices, actions, and interactions. Leaders who are clear about their values attract people who share their principles. If you value integrity, respect, and transparency, you're more likely to attract teammates who share those values.
- Consider the ideals you want your team to embody. Are you living by these values? By continually demonstrating your principles, you create a magnetic force that attracts others with similar beliefs.

2. Character & Integrity

- Your character establishes the tone for your team's culture. People are drawn to leaders who are sincere, honest, and dependable. When you maintain strong character, you inspire trust and loyalty, which attracts people who share those values.
- Leading with integrity is sticking to your word, treating others with dignity, and making decisions based on what is right rather than what is expedient. Your integrity becomes a light, attracting others who admire honest and honorable leadership.

3. Energy and Attitude

- Your enthusiasm and attitude towards your work as a leader have a significant impact on others around you. Positive, optimistic, and resilient leaders attract people who are both enthusiastic and solution-oriented. Leaders who continuously demonstrate pessimism or apathy, on the other hand, are more likely to attract followers who lack motivation and effort.
- Develop a positive, growth-oriented mindset. Approach obstacles with curiosity, not frustration, and demonstrate resilience in the face of setbacks. Your attitude will cause a ripple effect, influencing your team's energy and outlook.

4. Passion & Vision

- Leaders with a clear and compelling vision attract followers who share and are inspired by that vision. Your enthusiasm for the purpose strengthens your influence and attracts others who share your devotion. Passionate leaders inspire others by instilling a feeling of purpose and direction.
- Convey your goal and show your commitment to it via your actions. When others witness your steadfast dedication, they are more likely to connect their efforts with your objective and follow your example.

5. Communication and Connection

- Effective communication is essential for establishing connections and appealing to others. Leaders who are personable, compassionate, and authentic in their relationships build trust and rapport. When individuals feel heard and understood, they are more inclined to gravitate towards your leadership.
- Engage in active listening and endeavor to understand the opinions and needs of others. By engaging on a human level and talking honestly, you may foster an environment in which people feel appreciated and driven

to participate.

Reflection of Your Leadership on Your Team

Your team reflects who you are as a leader. If you're having trouble attracting the proper people, it could indicate that there's room for personal development. Examine your values, personality, energy, and vision. Are there any areas where you could improve to become the type of leader who draws and inspires others?

Nelson Mandela's leadership provides an amazing example of the Law of Magnetism. His unrelenting devotion to justice, integrity, and togetherness drew in supporters who shared his vision and determination. Mandela's attitude, enthusiasm, and resilience drew others who shared his vision for social transformation and healing.

Reflection: Are you attracting the people you want to lead?

Consider whether you are attracting the people you want to lead, or if there are gaps between your leadership style and the traits of those around you. Leadership necessitates continual self-reflection and development. The better you become, the more powerful the individuals you attract.

Action Step:

This week, select one attribute that you would like to see more of in your team, such as integrity, passion, or resilience. Concentrate on expressing that characteristic via your behaviors, decisions, and conversations. Pay attention to how your conscious effort affects the behavior and attitudes of those around you.

How Personal Growth Magnifies Leadership

"Leadership ability determines a person's level of effectiveness." — John C. Maxwell

Every leader has limitations personal, professional, or situational that might limit their effectiveness. The Law of the Lid asserts that a leader's effectiveness is measured by their ability to grow and overcome limits. In other words, as your capability increases, so does your ability to lead. If you want to advance your leadership and motivate others to do the same, you must continually invest in your own personal development.

Understanding the Lid of Your Leadership

Consider your leadership abilities to be like a jar lid. This lid regulates how much influence, success, and impact you may store in the jar. No matter how talented your team is or how good your goals are, your leadership skills limits your success. Therefore, the key to raising the lid is personal progress.

The best leaders recognise that their development never stops. They are constantly pushing themselves to improve their abilities, thinking, and understanding, which increases their ability to lead more effectively. By doing so, they increase their leadership influence and open up new chances for themselves and their teams.

Why Personal Growth Improves Leadership

1. Increased self-awareness

- Self-awareness is the first step towards personal growth. Leaders who understand their own talents, shortcomings, and blind spots may lead with humility and honesty. They are open to receiving feedback, eager to learn, and committed to self-improvement. This self-awareness enables

people to make conscious decisions that are consistent with their values and aims.
- Self-aware leaders instill trust and respect, fostering an environment in which people feel comfortable growing alongside them. By identifying and fighting to overcome their own limits, these leaders offer a strong example for those they serve.

2. Expanded skills and capabilities

- Personal and professional development broadens your skills and talents. Leaders that prioritise growth are more adaptable, imaginative, and adept at overcoming problems. This enlarged skill set not only improves your own performance, but also puts you in a better position to help and mentor others.
- Continuous learning is critical for leaders who wish to remain relevant and influential. Whether it's through reading, attending workshops, seeking mentorship, or obtaining new experiences, deliberate growth prepares you to take on larger responsibilities and lead with confidence.

3. Broader Perspective and Vision

- Personal development broadens and enhances your perception of the world around you. Leaders with a growth mentality are more receptive to fresh ideas, different perspectives, and unusual solutions. This transparency enables them to make better judgements and drive creativity in their workforce.
- A larger viewpoint enables you to connect with others on a deeper level. As you mature, you become more compassionate, inclusive, and culturally aware—qualities that are essential for developing solid relationships and maintaining a great team culture.

4. Enhanced Resilience and Emotional Intelligence

- Personal development fosters resilience by helping you develop the mental and emotional strength to deal with setbacks and obstacles. Leaders that are committed to growth are better able to deal with stress, manage conflict, and keep their cool in stressful times. This resilience benefits not only you, but also those you lead, instilling confidence and stability.
- Furthermore, personal development improves emotional intelligence (EQ), which is required for effective leadership. Leaders with high EQ are adept at understanding and managing their own emotions, as well as empathising with others. Emotional intelligence promotes trust, collaboration, and a positive team atmosphere.

5. Increased influence and impact

- Your impact grows as you do. Leaders who engage in their own development exude confidence, competence, and credibility. They attract and motivate others who share their drive for growth and achievement. Your personal development path inspires and encourages those around you, increasing your leadership impact.
- By consistently increasing your leadership lid, you foster a culture of continuous development and high expectations. Your team sees your commitment to improvement and is motivated to follow suit, resulting in collective progress and achievement.

The Ripple Effect of Personal Growth

The impact of personal development goes far beyond the individual. Leaders who commit to growth produce a ripple effect that affects their team, organisation, and even their community. A leader that prioritises growth not only enhances their own leadership, but also helps others grow and thrive.

Consider the leadership of Mahatma Gandhi. Gandhi's personal development journey, which included self-discipline, reflection, and learning, moulded his leadership and influence. His unrelenting dedication to nonviolence, ethics, and personal mastery drew and inspired millions, sparking a movement that altered a country.

Reflection: Are You Committed to Growing as a Leader?

Ask yourself: Am I actively seeking personal development, or am I allowing complacency to limit my leadership? Leadership is about committing to progress rather than striving for perfection. By raising your lid, you open up new possibilities for yourself and those you lead.

Action Step:

This week, choose one area of personal improvement to work on, such as self-awareness, resilience, or communication skills. Set a particular goal and take practical efforts to improve in that area. Consider how this dedication to progress affects both your effectiveness and the involvement of people you lead.

III

Part 3: Achieving Results through Leadership

7

Chapter 7: The Law of Navigation

Charting a Clear Path Forward

"Anyone can steer the ship, but it takes a leader to chart the course."
— John C. Maxwell

Great leaders do more than just lead; they navigate. According to the Law of Navigation, leaders must be able to design a clear course, anticipate challenges, and direct their teams to success. The capacity to perceive the larger picture, plan strategically, and communicate guidance effectively distinguishes exceptional leaders.

Navigating is about understanding where you're going, why it matters, and how to get there. A good leader provides clarity, confidence, and a sense of purpose to those he or she leads. This clear direction not only encourages people to move forward but also promotes resilience when faced with adversity.

The Importance of Establishing a Clear Path

Leadership without a clear direction is akin to navigating a ship without a compass. When the destination is unknown, confusion and ambiguity can soon arise, resulting in wasted effort, low morale, and missed opportunities. A clear-sighted leader, on the other hand, gives a road map that directs decision-making, aligns efforts, and inspires devotion.

Effective navigation entails not just plotting a plan but also adapting to changing circumstances and guiding the team through challenges. It necessitates strategic thinking, proactive planning, and articulating a vision that people can rally around.

Principles for Effective Navigation

1. Know where you are going

- The first step in navigating is to have a clear idea of where you're heading. Leaders must present a compelling vision that specifies the destination and explains why it matters. This vision guides the path, giving it purpose and meaning.
- Take some time to ponder about your mission and goals. Communicate this vision with clarity and passion, assisting your team in understanding not only the 'what' and the 'why.' When people believe in the final goal, they are more driven to face the hardships of the route.

2. Plan strategically

- Navigation is more than simply knowing where you want to go; it is also about finding out how to get there. Strategic planning entails recognizing critical milestones, predicting potential challenges, and establishing actionable strategies to move forward. Effective leaders anticipate potential impediments and address them ahead of time.

CHAPTER 7: THE LAW OF NAVIGATION

- Break down your vision into specific, attainable goals, and build a roadmap outlining the trip. Be clear about timeframes, resources, and responsibilities while being adaptable enough to change the plan as new information or obstacles emerge.

3. Anticipate obstacles and challenges

- Every path confronts challenges, and good leaders anticipate them before they occur. By proactively recognizing potential issues, you can create contingency plans and prepare your team for what comes next. This foresight mitigates the impact of setbacks while keeping the team focused on the goal.
- Take the time to evaluate potential risks and problems. Consider numerous circumstances and decide how you will respond. Prepare your team mentally and logistically so that they are ready to face challenges with resilience and confidence.

4. Communicate the plan

- Clear communication is critical for successful navigation. A well-defined plan loses its effectiveness if it is not adequately conveyed to all parties concerned. Leaders must ensure that all team members understand their roles, responsibilities, and general plan.
- When explaining the plan, be open about your expectations, timetables, and any roadblocks. Use plain, practical language, and check in frequently to provide updates and answer queries. When people feel educated and included, they are more likely to stick with the journey.

5. Lead by example

- Effective navigation entails more than simply planning and directing; it also requires setting a good example. Your behaviors must be consistent with the course you've charted. If you want your team to remain focused,

motivated, and resilient, you must continuously display those attributes.
- Demonstrate your dedication to the vision via your actions, decisions, and behavior. When your team sees your commitment, they are more inclined to trust your guidance and follow your lead with confidence.

Navigating Challenges With Confidence

Leadership is more than just charting a plan; it is also about guiding the team through adversity and disappointments. When presented with difficulty, exceptional leaders display resilience and adaptation while maintaining a steady hand and a clear focus on the end goal. By remaining cool and proactive, you may instill confidence in the people you lead.

Consider the leadership of Ernest Shackleton, who led the disastrous Endurance mission to Antarctica in 1914. When the ship became stranded in ice and the operation faced disaster, Shackleton's navigation abilities were put to the ultimate test. Despite the horrible circumstances, he remained focused on survival and led his crew through unprecedented adversity. Shackleton's ability to adapt, communicate, and lead with resolution saved the lives of all of the crew members, proving the need for clear and confident navigation.

Reflection: Are You Setting a Clear Path for Your Team?

Ask yourself: Do I have a clear vision of where I want to take my team, and am I effectively conveying that vision? Are there any roadblocks I've overlooked or strategic changes I need to make? To stay on track, it's important to constantly examine and adapt your navigation.

Action Step:

Take action this week by reviewing your present vision and strategic plan. Identify one area where you can add clarity or foresee potential issues. Communicate your findings to your team, and make any necessary changes to your strategy. Notice how this effort boosts your team's confidence and attention.

Guiding Others through Challenges

"Leaders become great not because of their power, but because of their ability to empower others." — John C. Maxwell

Every leader has challenges, but a great leader can help others overcome them with confidence, resilience, and clarity. The Law of Navigation underlines that leadership is more than just making the journey; it is also about safely and skillfully guiding others through tough waters.

Challenges are inescapable in any leadership route, whether in the form of external crises, internal debates, or unexpected failures. In difficult circumstances, true leaders step up, providing advice, confidence, and hope to their teams. Getting through problems requires vision, strategic thinking, empathy, and the courage to adapt.

Why Guiding Others through Challenges Is Crucial

When the path ahead becomes uncertain, people instinctively look to their leaders for direction and support. During these times, your team requires more than just a plan; they also need a leader who can stay calm, and focused, and deliver clarity in the middle of chaos. The way you respond to challenges affects not only the outcome but also the trust and loyalty of those under your leadership.

Empathy, resilience, and confidence are all required when leading others through problems. To successfully navigate challenges while keeping your team connected and engaged, you must find a balance between strategic foresight and emotional intelligence.

Principles for Leading Through Challenges

1. Recognize the truth and remain honest

- Recognizing the truth of the problem is the first step toward overcoming hurdles. Great leaders don't sugarcoat difficult situations or avoid uncomfortable truths. Instead, they are open about the problems they confront and communicate honestly with their coworkers. Transparency fosters trust and encourages an open, accountable culture.
- When confronted with a difficulty, be the first to reply honestly, explaining what is happening, what is at risk, and why it is significant. Accepting reality demonstrates genuineness and lays the foundation for collaborative problem resolution.

2. Maintain your calmness and confidence

- People typically seek guidance from their leaders during difficult times. If you panic, overreact, or display cynicism, your colleagues are likely to follow suit. Even in tough times, effective leaders maintain their composure and demonstrate confidence. This does not suggest ignoring problems, but rather tackling them with a calm and solution-oriented demeanor.
- Focus on remaining calm, grounded, and present. Allow your demeanor to demonstrate that you are capable of handling the situation and that your team can rely on your leadership. This tranquility instills confidence and stability, which are essential during times of uncertainty.

3. Adapt and strategize

- Leaders must often pivot and change their strategies in reaction to setbacks. What worked before may not be effective in a new or changing environment. Being willing to alter, reevaluate your strategy, and devise

new ideas is critical for overcoming obstacles.
- Take a step back to examine the issue and consider alternate solutions. Engage your team in brainstorming and decision-making to build a sense of ownership and collaboration. Being adaptive and open to change demonstrates how difficulties may be leveraged to create growth and innovation.

4. Communicate clear, actionable steps

- When presented with a challenge, people want clarity and advice. Effective leaders not only acknowledge the reality of the situation but also provide concrete and actionable answers for going forward. These stages serve as a road map, allowing your team to remain focused and unified even in challenging circumstances.
- Divide the challenge into smaller jobs, and clearly define each person's role and responsibilities. Keep your communication brief and detailed, and follow up on a regular basis to provide updates and address any concerns. This simple direction avoids confusion and keeps everyone on track.

5. Emphasise and foster resilience

- Problem-solving requires emotional support and encouragement in addition to strategic strategy. People may feel overwhelmed, anxious, or dejected, and it is your role as a leader to empathize with these emotions and promote resilience. Recognize your team's efforts, recognize their challenges, and provide words of encouragement.
- Create an environment in which people feel comfortable sharing their difficulties and seeking assistance. Encourage a resilient mindset by acknowledging small triumphs and emphasizing that failure is a natural part of the journey. When people feel supported and understood, they are more likely to remain involved and motivated.

Resilience in Action: Winston Churchill's Leadership

Winston Churchill's leadership during World War II is one of the best-known examples of assisting people in difficult times. Despite seemingly overwhelming conditions, Winston Churchill's unwavering commitment, strategic acumen, and great communication kept the British people together and resilient. He did not overlook the awful realities of war, but rather provided unambiguous leadership, motivated the populace, and instilled hope.

Churchill's leadership illustrates the need to be honest about challenges, maintain composure, adapt approaches, and inspire others to be resilient. His ability to guide his country through one of history's worst periods is a spectacular example of the Law of Navigation in action.

Reflection: How Do You Lead People Through Difficulties?

Ask yourself: When faced with a challenge, do I remain calm, speak clearly, and empathize with those I lead? Are there any ways I can improve my ability to negotiate barriers and provide clear direction?

Action Step:

This week, identify a potential challenge that your team is presently experiencing or will encounter shortly. Take the time to strategize, design specific steps, and communicate your aim. Maintain a calm and encouraging demeanor, and see how it influences your team's confidence and resilience.

8

Chapter 8: The Law of Victory

Leaders Find a Way to Win

"Victory is always possible for the person who refuses to stop fighting." — Napoleon Hill

When the stakes are great and the chances appear stacked against you, it's easy to become discouraged or question your objective. However, exceptional leaders recognize that winning is more than just having a smart strategy; it is also about having an unshakeable determination to succeed. According to the Law of Victory, leaders find a way to win because they are motivated by a deep commitment to the objective and the people they lead.

True leadership does not mean never failing; rather, it means refusing to accept defeat as the final consequence. Leaders with a victory mindset do not focus on hurdles or blame others. Instead, they focus on solutions, mobilize their teams, and motivate everyone to overcome the obstacles they encounter. They are unwavering in their pursuit of the objective, believing that success is always possible, no matter how arduous the route.

The Power of a Victory Mindset

What distinguishes successful leaders is not chance or favorable circumstances; it is their thinking. They see setbacks as opportunities to develop, perfect their approach, and demonstrate their resilience. They are tenacious, resourceful, and determined, and they encourage others to adopt the same winning mindset.

A victory mindset does not imply ignoring challenges or claiming that every setback is unimportant. It entails accepting reality, learning from failures, and identifying new paths forward. When a leader embraces this approach, they foster an environment of resilience, inventiveness, and collaborative determination.

Principles of Achieving Victory

1. Commitment to Mission

- Victory begins with a firm dedication to the mission. Leaders who are sincerely committed to their mission inspire others to follow suit. This dedication is what drives perseverance when the going gets difficult. It is more than simply a superficial belief in success; it is a firm conviction that obtaining the goal is worth the effort.
- Take the time to explain the significance of your purpose and why it matters not just to you, but to those you lead. People are more inclined to face problems with resolve when they comprehend the greater significance of what they are working for.

2. Adaptability and Resourcefulness

- Winning leaders understand that the route to triumph is rarely straight. When faced with a stumbling block, they are willing to adjust their strategies, reconsider their objectives, and devise new solutions. This

adaptability is critical to success because it allows leaders to remain focused on the objective while responding to changing conditions.
- When challenges arise, reject the impulse to stick with a failing plan. Instead, gather your team, examine the situation, and brainstorm potential solutions. Encourage innovative problem solutions and emphasize that setbacks are a necessary part of the route to victory.

3. Inspiring and mobilizing the team

- A leader's victory is never accomplished alone. It demands the combined efforts of a dedicated and inspired team. Great leaders understand how to rally their teams, develop momentum, and maintain strong morale even in difficult situations. They provide a sense of purpose and belief in one's ability to succeed.
- Take the time to interact with your team, hear their issues, and provide support. Use clear and compelling communication to remind them of the mission and build a shared desire for triumph. When people feel appreciated and driven, they are more likely to go above and beyond to achieve their goals.

4. Perseverance and resilience

- Victory does not always occur swiftly or easily. It frequently involves long-term perseverance and tenacity in the face of adversity. Leaders who find a way to win are those who stick with it through the highs and lows, staying focused on the final objective even when progress appears slow.
- Develop resilience by keeping a long-term perspective and emphasizing the necessity of staying the course. Celebrate little triumphs along the road to keep the team motivated and remind them that each step is part of a bigger picture.

5. Taking responsibility for the outcome

- Winning leaders avoid making excuses or shifting blame. They accept all responsibility for the outcome, whether it is a success or failure. This responsibility fosters a culture of ownership and trust, enabling everyone to take their positions seriously and contribute their full potential.
- When faced with a setback, take ownership of the situation and lead the path towards finding answers. Show your team that mistakes and failures are opportunities to learn, adapt, and rebuild.

Victory in Action: Nelson Mandela's Leadership

Nelson Mandela's victory over apartheid in South Africa illustrates a leader's determination and resilience. Despite 27 years in prison, Mandela never lost sight of his vision of a free and equal country. Despite enormous personal sacrifice and long-standing political resistance, he remained committed to the cause of eradicating apartheid.

Mandela's leadership was about more than simply his perseverance; it was about rallying and inspiring people to believe in the prospect of change. His unwavering commitment, strategic agility, and ability to mobilize others around the cause eventually resulted in the demise of apartheid and the development of a new South Africa. Mandela's biography is a dramatic illustration of The Law of Victory in action.

Reflection: Do You Lead With a Victory Mindset?

Consider whether you are committed to your purpose even when faced with obstacles. Am I motivating my team and accepting full responsibility for the results? Leading with a victory mindset necessitates ongoing self-reflection and an openness to change.

Action Step:

This week, select a difficult circumstance or project you are currently dealing with. Take some time to rethink your strategy and examine other options. Reaffirm your dedication to the mission and share your reinvigorated resolve with your team. Consider how this restored concentration and clarity affects your team's motivation and morale.

The Unwavering Mindset of Success

"Success is not the result of one big leap, but of the small, consistent steps taken every day." — John C. Maxwell

One of the most important characteristics of good leaders is constancy. The Law of Consistency emphasizes that leadership success is founded on consistent, deliberate, and disciplined activities conducted daily. It is not the spectacular or grand actions that are most important, but rather the calm determination to stick with it no matter how difficult things become.

Success, particularly in leadership, is not by accident. It is the result of consistently doing the right things, even when motivation wanes, problems arise, or results are delayed. Successful leaders build an unshakeable mindset, one that values consistency over instant success and endurance over ease.

The Value of Consistency in Leadership

Consistency promotes trust. When individuals know their leader's actions are steady, reliable, and consistent, they feel more stable and secure. This trust is vital for good leadership because it tells people that the leader will remain devoted and focused in any situation.

Consistency also builds credibility. Leaders who continually exhibit their principles, vision, and devotion gain the respect and loyalty of the people they manage. People are more likely to follow someone they see as trustworthy, disciplined, and principled.

Principles of Consistency

1. Commit to daily discipline

- Success is the result of tiny efforts made persistently over time. This notion applies to leadership, where cultivating habits of excellence, tenacity, and honesty provides a firm foundation. Leaders who adhere to daily disciplines reinforce their mission and match their activities with their long-term objectives.
- Identify the tiny acts that will help you and your team grow, then commit to practicing them every day. Holding regular team check-ins, encouraging open communication, and setting a good example are all tiny acts that add up to make a big difference.

2. Stay true to your core values

- Regardless of the problems or temptations that come, consistent leaders remain grounded in their underlying convictions. They do not give up their values for short-term benefit or take the easy way out. This steadfast commitment to their beliefs instills a strong sense of honesty and trustworthiness.
- Define your essential values and revisit them frequently. Make sure your behaviors reflect these principles and lead by example in both minor and large decisions. Allow your values to guide you when faced with difficult decisions.

3. Develop a long-term perspective

- Consistency necessitates patience and a long-term outlook. Successful leaders recognize that meaningful results need time and consistent effort.

They don't get frustrated by minor setbacks or distracted by short-term trends. Instead, they prioritize steady, incremental growth.
- Cultivate a mindset that prioritizes long-term effects over instant gratification. When presented with a hurdle, remind yourself and your team of the larger picture and the ultimate goals you're striving for. This mindset keeps you grounded and resilient in the face of adversity.

4. Embrace the Power of Habit

- The most consistent leaders know how habits influence their actions and outcomes. They develop behaviors that reinforce their objective and keep them on track, even when their motivation varies. These behaviors instill a sense of discipline in leaders, allowing them to stay focused, motivated, and productive.
- Identify the habits that help you grow and thrive as a leader. Prioritise and incorporate them into your routine. Whether it's beginning each day with reflection, prioritizing work, or practicing thankfulness, these habits form the foundation of your constancy.

5. Measure progress and celebrate milestones

- Consistency does not imply neglecting the necessity of recognizing accomplishments. Successful leaders track progress regularly and recognize accomplishments by themselves and their teams. These moments of praise highlight the importance of persistent effort and keep the team encouraged to keep moving forward.
- Create a strategy for tracking progress and celebrating major milestones. Regularly assess how far you and your team have come and express gratitude for the effort and dedication required to get there. This acknowledgment promotes a culture of consistency and perseverance.

Consistency of Action: Leadership of Angela Merkel

Angela Merkel's stint as German Chancellor is a powerful example of the need for consistency in leadership. Merkel rose to prominence for her steady and pragmatic approach to governing during her 16-year tenure. She constantly followed her principles of reasoned decision-making, tenacity in the face of crises, and dedication to long-term stability.

During her tenure, Merkel faced numerous challenges, ranging from economic crises to political upheavals. Throughout it all, she remained a calm and dependable leader, earning the faith and respect of her country. Merkel's continuous acts, even during challenging times, bolstered her reputation and solidified her legacy as a steadfast and trustworthy leader.

Reflection: How Consistent is Your Leadership?

Ask yourself: Are my daily behaviors consistent with my values and mission? Am I developing the habits and discipline required to remain on the path even when obstacles arise? Consistency necessitates self-awareness and a dedication to intentional development.

Action Step:

This week, pick one tiny yet effective habit you may implement daily to improve your leadership consistency. It could be a habit related to personal development, teamwork, or strategic planning. Commit to continuously adopting this habit for the next 30 days, and track how it affects your thinking and leadership.

9

Chapter 9: The Law of the Big Picture

Seeing Beyond the Immediate

"The very essence of leadership is that you have a vision. It's got to be a vision you articulate clearly and forcefully on every occasion. You can't blow an uncertain trumpet." — Reverend Theodore M. Hesburgh

Great leaders have the rare ability to see beyond the present moment and see a future that does not yet exist. According to the Law of Goals, the most effective leaders have a clear and compelling vision of where they want to go and are adept at persuading others to see the same thing. They understand that people are inspired by the possibilities of tomorrow, not the work or obstacles of today.

Vision is the ability to see beyond what is seen now. It is about seeing the potential of people, projects, and opportunities, as well as aligning current actions with long-term objectives. Leaders who employ The Law of Vision communicate a sense of direction and purpose, motivating others to overcome obstacles and stay on track.

The Power of a Compelling Vision

A vision is more than just setting goals; it is about creating a narrative that gives meaning to each stage of the journey. A compelling vision justifies current sacrifices and efforts as investments in a brighter future. Leaders with a vision inspire optimism, increase confidence, and create momentum.

However, vision isn't enough by itself. It needs continual communication and alignment of goals and activities. When a leader's words and actions align with the vision they espouse, they gain credibility and the trust of those under their leadership.

Principles for looking beyond the immediate

1. Create a clear, compelling vision

- A leader's vision must be clear, precise, and purpose-driven. It should address fundamental problems such as "Where are we going?" Why does this matter? How will we get there? When people understand not only what they're working for, but also why it's important, they become more motivated and dedicated.
- Take the time to define your vision. It should be more than simply a distant goal; it should provide a clear image of what success looks like and why it is worth pursuing. Once defined, share it frequently and enthusiastically.

2. Align vision with action

- Vision is only effective if it is supported by coordinated actions. Leaders must ensure that their everyday decisions, actions, and activities reflect and reinforce the vision they have set. This alignment builds trust by exhibiting the leader's honesty and integrity.
- Evaluate your behaviors regularly to ensure that they are consistent with your goals. Are the approaches you're using helping you get closer to

your perfect future? If not, make the necessary adjustments to remain on track. Your consistency in aligning words and deeds builds credibility and motivates individuals to stay engaged.

3. Inspire and rally others around the vision

- A vision is powerful when it is shared and embraced by the people you lead. It is not enough for the leader to see it; everyone on the team must connect with it. Great leaders convey their vision in a way that inspires excitement, dedication, and a shared sense of purpose.
- Take advantage of every opportunity to express your perspective in a clear and relevant manner. Use stories, metaphors, and examples to paint a vivid picture of your desired future. Show your team how their roles fit into the bigger picture and what difference they're making.

4. Keep a long-term view

- Visionary leaders are unaffected by temporary setbacks or distractions. They keep their eyes on the big picture and help their teams stay focused, especially when faced with obstacles. This long-term perspective allows leaders to remain flexible and adaptable while acknowledging that short-term losses are unavoidable.
- When hurdles arise, remind yourself and your team of the greater vision. Encourage persistence by framing setbacks as necessary milestones toward your shared goals. The emphasis on the big picture keeps everyone motivated and resilient.

5. Develop a culture of vision-driven growth

- Leaders who succeed in seeing beyond the immediate understand the importance of creating a culture in which everyone is encouraged to contribute to and align with the vision. This includes promoting open communication, valuing many perspectives, and empowering others to

take ownership of the mission.
- Create an environment in which people feel comfortable sharing their ideas and perspectives on how to achieve the vision. Recognize and applaud contributions that advance the vision, and be open to refining it based on group expertise. When people feel appreciated and involved, they are more likely to make their ideas a reality.

Vision in Action: Walt Disney's Leadership

Walt Disney's trip demonstrates the ability to see beyond the immediate. In the early twentieth century, when animation was still a novelty, Disney saw a future in which animation was more than just a passing trend, but a powerful storytelling medium. His vision led to the creation of legendary animated films and creative theme parks that have inspired generations.

Disney's vision included more than just inventiveness; it also included the experience he wanted to offer to his audience. He passionately advocated for developing a sense of wonder, enchantment, and connection. Despite financial challenges and skepticism, Disney stayed committed to his aim, constantly linking his actions to the bigger vision. His vision and determination led to the establishment of one of the world's most recognizable entertainment organizations.

Reflection: Do you look beyond the immediate?

Do you have a clear and appealing vision for your leadership? Is my communication and actions in line with that vision? True leadership is not only having a vision but also cultivating a shared sense of purpose that drives collaborative growth.

CHAPTER 9: THE LAW OF THE BIG PICTURE

Action Step:

This week, create a clear and precise vision for the project or program you're leading. Communicate it to your team in a way that inspires them and illustrates why it is important. Take the time to listen to their perspectives and, if required, revise the concept. Consider how this clarity influences engagement and motivation.

Aligning Vision, Strategy, and Execution

"Vision without action is a daydream. Action without vision is a nightmare."
— Japanese Proverb

Vision is important in leadership, but it cannot be achieved on its own. The Law of Alignment states that in order for a leader to be effective, their vision must be carefully prepared and executed with accuracy. The most effective leaders ensure that their vision, strategy, and execution are perfectly matched. This connection transforms ideas into reality, plans into progress, and aspirations into successes.

Vision is about seeing what might be. Strategy is about determining how to get there. Execution is the process of taking the necessary actions to make something happen. When these three components work together, leaders build momentum and instill confidence in the people they lead. When they are disconnected, the vision becomes merely an aspiration, and the team struggles to remain motivated and engaged.

The Power of Alignment in Leadership

Alignment gives clarity and direction, ensuring that everyone understands not only the destination but also the route and steps required to get there. Leaders that thrive at alignment bridge the gap between the conceptual and the real. They have the discipline to turn great ideas into actual actions, as well as the foresight to adapt their methods when situations change.

Alignment generates synergy. When vision, strategy, and execution are in sync, they reinforce each other. The vision explains why, the strategy explains how, and the execution demonstrates the outcomes. Leaders who master alignment help their people stay focused, overcome obstacles, and achieve long-term success.

Principles of Aligning Vision, Strategy, and Execution

1. Define a Clear and Specific Vision

- It all starts with a clear and focused vision. This vision should provide a clear image of the future you want to create and why it is important. Your vision must be captivating enough to elicit commitment and specific enough to drive decision-making.
- Spend time refining your vision until it is clear, explicit, and purpose-driven. Make sure it resonates with your team and is consistent with your fundamental beliefs. A clear vision serves as the foundation for all that follows.

2. Develop a Strategic Plan

- Vision without a plan is equivalent to a destination without a map. Once you have a clear vision, create a strategic plan outlining the major milestones, goals, and resources required to realize it. This strategy should break down the journey into small steps, providing a clear path forward.
- Work with your team to develop a strategic plan that includes short-term objectives, key performance indicators, and contingency measures. Ensure that everyone understands their respective roles and responsibilities within the strategy.

3. Create a culture of accountability

- Accountability is required at all levels to ensure alignment. Leaders must set clear expectations and constantly review progress to ensure that everyone is adhering to the strategy. When failures occur, accountability enables leaders to respond quickly and keep the team on target.
- Create a culture in which accountability is seen as a tool for progress rather than a punishment. Encourage open communication and provide regular feedback to keep the team engaged and focused on the purpose.

4. Empower and equip your team

- For execution to succeed, leaders must provide their teams with the resources, skills, and autonomy they require to execute at their peak. Alignment is more than simply having the correct plan; it is also about having the appropriate people in the right positions and providing them with the resources they need to succeed.
- Invest in training, tools, and development to support your team's growth and success. Encourage autonomy by allowing your staff to take responsibility for their tasks while yet giving direction and support as needed.

5. Adjust and adapt as necessary

- Successful leaders recognize that situations change, and so do their plans. Alignment does not imply rigidity; it involves being malleable while remaining committed to the vision. When new information or challenges surface, leaders must be willing to rethink and realign their plans.
- Regularly review progress and remain open to making changes. Encourage flexibility among your team members, emphasizing that adaptability is critical for long-term success.

Alignment in Action: The Leadership of Indra Nooyi

Indra Nooyi, former CEO of PepsiCo, is an excellent example of a leader who understands The Law of Alignment. When she took over as CEO, she had a clear strategy for PepsiCo: to focus on long-term growth through healthier products and investments in environmental sustainability. Nooyi created a strategic plan called "Performance with Purpose," which listed major objectives such as product innovation, environmental impact, and community support.

Under her leadership, the organization not only set high goals but also carried them out with thorough preparation and alignment at all levels. Nooyi continually conveyed her vision, made sure strategic decisions mirrored it, and held everyone responsible for it. Her convergence of vision, strategy, and execution changed PepsiCo and cemented the company's global reputation as responsible and inventive.

Reflection: Are Your Vision, Strategy, and Execution Aligned?

Ask yourself if your vision, strategy, and execution are clear and consistent. Are your activities compatible with your vision and strategic priorities? Effective leadership is not only having a goal but also coordinating everything you do to achieve it.

Action Step:

This week, assess your present vision and strategic plan. Identify any areas where alignment may be lacking and develop a detailed action plan to close the gaps. Consider soliciting feedback from your team to improve your plan and strengthen alignment. Consider the effect of these changes on your team's focus and engagement.

IV

Part 4: Building Lasting Influence and Legacy

10

Chapter 10: The Law of Timing

Understanding When to Act

"**The right decision at the wrong time is the wrong decision.**" — Dr. Tony Evans

Timing is crucial in leadership. Knowing what to do isn't enough; you also need to know when to do it. The Law of Timing emphasizes that a leader's effectiveness is frequently determined by their ability to detect the best times to act. In leadership, doing the right thing at the wrong time may stymie progress, erode trust, and derail a goal.

Great leaders are aware of the requirements, readiness, and context of their environment. They carefully appraise situations, knowing when patience is required and when prompt action is required. They understand that timing can affect not only the outcome of an activity but also the morale and confidence of their team. The Law of Timing is about leading with awareness and intentionality, understanding your organization's rhythm, and making decisions based on that understanding.

The Power of Proper Timing in Leadership

Timing is more than just patience; it is also about being perceptive. Leaders who grasp the art of timing understand their surroundings and recognize opportunities. They recognize that timing can mean the difference between success and failure, progress and stagnation, or motivation and discouragement.

Leaders with excellent timing listen, observe, and respond. They do not make hasty decisions out of fear, nor do they put off taking action because they are too comfortable. Instead, they build the insight to act when the time is right, using timing as a strategic advantage.

Principles for Understanding When to Act

1. Read about the situation and the individuals involved

- Effective timing necessitates a thorough awareness of the circumstances and the individuals affected by your decisions. Before acting, leaders must acquire information, listen to their teams, and assess their readiness. This understanding enables leaders to determine whether the time is appropriate for a change, decision, or effort.
- Stay connected to your team and environment to improve your situational awareness. Pay attention to the emotions, energy levels, and feedback of those you lead. Recognize that timing is more than simply logistics; it is also about recognizing your team's overall mood and readiness.

2. Balance Urgency and Patience

- Timing necessitates finding a balance between urgency and patience. Leaders who act with urgency without rushing show that they value capturing opportunities while remaining mindful of potential hazards. Patient leaders without procrastinating demonstrate that they respect

rigorous planning and prevent unnecessary delays.
- What is the cost of waiting? What are the risks of acting too soon? Weigh these considerations and establish a sense of urgency combined with thoughtful patience. This balance promotes trust and ensures that your decisions are deliberate but timely.

3. Observe the bigger picture

- Understanding the bigger picture of your activities is often necessary for effective timing. Leaders who focus solely on immediate results may overlook the long-term consequences of their actions. The best leaders see the broad picture and act with a vision that goes beyond the present moment.
- Before making any critical decisions, take the time to zoom out and see the big picture. Consider how your timing affects not only the present circumstance but also future goals and relationships. This broad view enables you to lead with foresight and intention.

4. Cultivate flexibility and adaptability

- Even the greatest plans might be altered owing to unanticipated circumstances. Leaders who excel in time remain adaptable, understanding that being strict about timing can lead to missed opportunities. They are open to new knowledge and are willing to change their plans as needed.
- Encourage adaptability in both yourself and your team. Communicate that timing is not always predictable, and that it is sometimes better to change than to insist. This adaptability promotes resilience and prepares your team to face unexpected situations.

5. Evaluate and Learn from Timing Mistakes

- No leader has perfect timing every time. Learning to master timing necessitates a willingness to examine previous decisions, admit faults, and modify accordingly. Leaders who are open about timing blunders obtain significant insights that will help them improve their judgment in the future.

- Reflect on previous decisions and find situations where timing was critical. What have you learned from these experiences? How will you improve your sense of timing in the future? This dedication to self-reflection increases your leadership effectiveness over time.

Timing of Action: Leadership of Abraham Lincoln

Abraham Lincoln's leadership during the Civil War exhibits the Law of Timing. Lincoln was under intense pressure to move decisively on the problem of slavery, and he knew that the timing of his actions would have a huge impact on the country. Despite his convictions, Lincoln carefully considered the political, military, and social context before issuing the Emancipation Proclamation.

Lincoln understood that moving too quickly would result in backlash, splitting the Union and undermining the war effort. On the other side, lingering too long may stifle the moral and strategic impetus required to garner support. Lincoln's declaration transformed the trajectory of the war and reshaped the nation's identity by timing it perfectly. His sense of time exhibited patience, vision, and the ability to seize a critical moment.

Reflection: Are You Leading at the Right Time?

Ask yourself: Do I routinely think about the timing of my actions? Am I conscious of the influence my decisions have on the people I lead, and do I strike a balance between hurry and patience? Mastering timing entails generating the appropriate conditions and acting with intention, rather than waiting for the ideal moment.

Action Step:

This week, identify an impending choice or action that necessitates precise time. Take the time to gather information, appraise the issue, and determine your team's readiness. Make a conscious plan for when and how to respond, and then track the impact of your timing on outcomes and morale.

Balancing Patience and Urgency

"Patience is not the absence of action; it is timing. It waits on the right time to act, for the right principles, and in the right way." — Fulton J. Sheen

Great leadership necessitates balancing two seemingly opposing characteristics: patience and hurry. The Law of Balance explains that while urgency motivates development and action, patience ensures that those activities are smart, purposeful, and long-lasting. Leaders who understand this balance foster settings where momentum and mindfulness coexist, resulting in consistent and deliberate growth.

Impatience can cause rash decisions, burnout, and strained relationships. However, excessive patience can lead to missed chances, stagnation, and indecision. The most effective leaders cultivate the knowledge to know when to move forward and when to pause. The Law of Balance is about recognizing this dynamic and leading in a way that balances forward energy and cautious contemplation.

The Power of Balance in Leadership

Finding the right mix between patience and urgency enables leaders to respond to difficulties with a steady hand. Leaders who strike this balance foster a culture of progress and calm, in which their staff are motivated to act while also trusting that their leader is methodical and thoughtful.

This balance enables leaders to maintain focus, prevent avoidable setbacks, and keep their teams on track with the purpose. It's about making clear and confident decisions, and understanding when to accelerate and when to back off.

Principles to Balance Patience and Urgency

1. Identify Critical Priorities

- Balancing patience and urgency requires leaders to have a clear sense of what is most essential. Not every problem requires urgent attention, and not every decision necessitates waiting. Leaders must identify the important priorities that propel their vision ahead and address them with urgency while remaining patient in other areas.
- Make a priority list that includes the most time-sensitive and important tasks. Communicate these priorities to your team, then allocate resources accordingly. By focusing your urgency on what is most important, you avoid spreading your energy thinly.

2. Cultivate situational awareness

- Leaders who strike a balance between patience and haste have good situational awareness. They carefully consider the circumstances and timing of each decision, recognizing when external forces or team readiness necessitate quick action or cautious waiting.
- Create the practice of periodically reviewing the circumstance and asking yourself, "Is this the right time to act?" What are the implications of moving too fast or too slowly? This awareness allows you to make better educated, balanced decisions.

3. Communicate clearly and transparently

- The balance of patience and urgency applies to how leaders interact with

their staff. Leaders must communicate clearly when urgency is required and explain why patience is necessary in other cases. This transparency promotes trust and avoids confusion or misalignment.
- Explain your reasoning to your staff to foster open communication. When advocating immediate action, express the urgency and importance. When demonstrating patience, emphasize the need to wait and the advantages of taking a controlled approach.

4. Stay True to Your Core Values

- When leaders stay true to their core beliefs, they are better equipped to strike a balance between patience and haste. Values serve as a compass for decision-making, allowing leaders to resist the temptation to haste or delay based only on external demands.
- Reflect on your core values and make your behaviors consistent with them. Ask yourself whether moving immediately or waiting is consistent with your values and objectives. This foundation ensures that your choices are principled and consistent.

5. Practice Emotional Regulation

- Impatience is generally caused by internal pressure, anxiety, or a drive to prove oneself. Leaders who strike a balance between patience and urgency have learned to control their emotions, making judgments from a state of clarity rather than reaction. Emotional control enables leaders to remain calm in challenging situations.
- Increase your self-awareness by understanding the causes that create impatience or reluctance. Use mindfulness practices to stay focused and tackle each scenario with a calm and clear mind. Emotional management enables you to respond deliberately rather than impulsively.

Balance in Action: Leadership of Angela Merkel

Angela Merkel, the former Chancellor of Germany, demonstrates the Law of Balance. During her term, Merkel encountered various crises, including economic and humanitarian ones. Her leadership style was distinguished by a unique capacity to mix patience and urgency. Merkel tackled complex issues with caution, gathering information, consulting experts, and weighing various viewpoints before making judgments.

At the same time, Merkel understood when immediate action was required, such as during the European financial crisis and the 2015 refugee crisis. Her actions were immediate and decisive, but they were also the result of careful planning and strategic thinking. Merkel's balance of patience and urgency enabled her to guide Germany through difficult times while retaining stability and trust.

Reflection: Are You Balancing Patience and Urgency in Your Leadership?

Ask yourself: Do I know when to act quickly and when to be patient? Am I striking a balance that encourages both advancement and stability in my team? Leadership is more than just pushing forward; it is about leading with awareness, discernment, and purpose.

Action Step:

This week, find an area in your leadership where you experience a conflict between haste and patience. Take the time to examine the issue and develop situational awareness. Make a determined decision to proceed in a hurry or with patience, based on the needs of the moment and the overall picture.

11

Chapter 11: The Law of Legacy

Leadership's Greatest Reward: Leaving a Legacy

"**The greatest use of life is to spend it on something that will outlast it.**" — William James

True leadership is assessed not by a leader's accomplishments during their tenure, but by the long-term impact they leave. The Law of Legacy emphasizes that a leader's ultimate success is defined by their capacity to leave a significant and lasting legacy. Leadership is about more than simply the present moment; it is about leaving a legacy that will last long after you are gone.

Every decision, deed, and relationship that a leader cultivates helps to shape their legacy. Leaders who inspire others to carry out their vision are more impactful than those who only achieve short-term goals. The Law of Legacy says that leadership is about sowing seeds for the future and leading those you lead to build on the foundation you've laid.

The Power of Legacy in Leadership

When leaders concentrate on leaving a legacy, their focus shifts from immediate accomplishment to long-term effect. A legacy-driven leader intentionally shapes their organization, team, and culture. They recognize that their influence goes beyond their tenure and strive to guarantee that their beliefs, vision, and values are passed down to future generations.

Legacy-minded leaders invest in creating future leaders, empowering them to continue the job they started, rather than focusing solely on their leadership journey. This approach lifts leadership from selfish desire to selfless service, ensuring that the organization's mission and values thrive even in their absence.

Principles for Leaving A Leadership Legacy

1. Live with purpose and intention

- Leaving a legacy begins with living and leading purposefully. Leaders who are committed to a defined mission leave an enduring impact. They regularly reflect on their beliefs and ensure their leadership decisions are founded on those values.
- Consider the objective behind your leadership. What do you hope to be remembered for? How do your current actions contribute to the future you want to create? Living with intention guarantees that your leadership has a long-term impact.

2. Develop and Mentor Future Leaders

- One of the most effective ways to leave a lasting legacy is to invest in the next generation of leaders. Leaders who mentor and develop others spread their knowledge, wisdom, and ideals. This creates continuity and guarantees that the organization's mission is sustainable.

- Identify prospective leaders on your team and engage in their development. Share your experiences, lessons learned, and thoughts with them. Empower people to take responsibility for their responsibilities and equip them to lead with honesty and purpose.

3. Develop a culture of growth and learning

- Legacy-driven CEOs prioritize fostering a culture of growth and ongoing learning. They understand that the value of their legacy is contingent on the strength of the organization or team they leave behind. By establishing a culture that values invention, collaboration, and progress, they ensure that their influence lasts long after they are gone.
- Create a culture that supports curiosity, adaptation, and personal development. Encourage your team to challenge themselves, learn new things, and embrace change. This growth-oriented approach will cement your legacy as a leader who helped others succeed.

4. Act with integrity and consistency

- A legacy is based on trust, which is acquired through integrity and consistency. Leaders who stick to their values even when things get tough leave a lasting impression. Their actions are consistent with their words, and they lead with integrity and transparency.
- Consistently uphold your beliefs in all situations, and set a good example of leadership for others. Acting with integrity earns you a long-lasting reputation, ensuring that your influence continues to inspire and guide others.

5. Prioritize long-term outcomes over short-term gains

- Leaders who leave a legacy value long-term sustainability over short-term success. They resist the desire to seek fast triumphs that may jeopardize future success. Instead, they prioritize actions that lay a solid

foundation for future growth and success.
- Examine your choices through the perspective of long-term consequences. Consider how this decision will affect the organization five, 10, or twenty years from now. By focusing on long-term growth and your organization's health, you may leave a lasting legacy.

Legacy in Action: Nelson Mandela's Leadership

Nelson Mandela's leadership legacy is one of the most powerful illustrations of The Law of Legacy. Mandela's devotion to equality, justice, and reconciliation helped shape South Africa's transformation from an apartheid-torn society to one striving for unity and peace. His impact continues to influence leaders all across the world even after he left office.

Mandela knew that leadership is about more than just personal achievement; it is about creating a future that benefits others. His emphasis on forgiveness and nation-building had an enduring impact not only on South Africa but also on world leadership. Mandela's legacy demonstrates the power of selfless leadership and the importance of leaving a better society for future generations.

Reflection: What legacy will you leave?

Consider: What do I want my leadership legacy to be? How am I investing in the future with my actions today? The legacy you leave is more than just your successes during your tenure; it is also about the long-term impact you establish through your vision, values, and relationships.

Action Step:

This week, reflect on your leadership legacy. Identify one area where you can invest in the development of future leaders or improve your organization's long-term viability. Take deliberate steps to ensure that your leadership leaves a positive and enduring impression.

CHAPTER 11: THE LAW OF LEGACY

Building a Sustainable Culture of Leadership

"Culture eats strategy for breakfast." — Peter Drucker

Leaders come and go, but culture persists. The Law of Culture emphasizes the importance of creating an atmosphere in which leadership can go beyond the individual and become a common way of thinking, behaving, and influencing. Leaders who construct a lasting leadership culture leave a legacy that is not attached to a single individual, but rather to the concepts, values, and practices that empower everyone in the organization.

A sustainable leadership culture is one in which everyone feels empowered and inspired to lead in their unique style. It's a culture based on trust, a common vision, ongoing learning, and a real dedication to the objective. Leaders that prioritize culture recognize that their influence is not achieved by being the loudest voice in the room, but by establishing an environment in which everyone feels appreciated and empowered to contribute.

The Power of Culture in Leadership

Culture is an invisible force that determines an organization's behavior, choices, and connections. A strong leadership culture ensures that the organization's ideals and values are not only dependent on one leader. Instead, they get woven into the fabric of the organization, impacting every decision and activity.

When leaders invest in developing a sustainable culture, they foster an atmosphere in which employees are inspired to learn, innovate, and collaborate. This culture becomes the cornerstone for long-term success, guiding the organization through transitions and obstacles.

Principles for Building a Sustainable Culture of Leadership

1. Lead by Example and Set Clear Expectations

- A sustainable culture begins with leaders who model the behaviors and values they wish to see in others. Leaders who lead by example establish the benchmark for integrity, teamwork, and accountability. They set clear expectations that are consistent with the organization's mission and values, ensuring that everyone understands their role in fostering the culture.
- Consider how your activities connect with the culture you wish to create. Are you demonstrating the ideals you wish to see in others? Communicate your expectations clearly and consistently, supporting behaviors that promote a healthy and sustainable culture.

2. Empower and Trust Your Team

- Culture grows when individuals feel trusted and empowered to lead. Leaders who promote a leadership culture empower their teams to take responsibility for their responsibilities, make decisions, and contribute ideas. This empowerment not only boosts confidence but also fosters a sense of collective responsibility for the organization's success.
- Create opportunities for your team to take on leadership responsibilities, regardless of their position or experience. Demonstrate your trust in their judgment by delegating meaningful responsibilities and fostering initiative. Empowered team members actively contribute to the leadership culture.

3. Encourage open communication and feedback

- Open, honest, and transparent communication is essential for fostering a sustainable leadership culture. Leaders must foster an environment in

which feedback can flow easily in all ways (up, down, and across). This openness promotes trust, innovation, and ongoing progress.
- Create regular avenues of contact, such as team meetings, one-on-one check-ins, and anonymous feedback tools. Encourage your team members to share their ideas, concerns, and suggestions. By emphasizing open communication, you foster a culture of growth and collaboration.

4. Celebrate success and learn from failure

- Leaders who foster sustainable cultures acknowledge and reward their team's accomplishments. They recognize that acknowledgment and gratitude are critical for sustaining motivation and engagement. At the same time, they see failure as an opportunity for progress rather than a reason to blame.
- Make it a habit to celebrate individual and team accomplishments. Recognize not only the outcomes but also the effort and dedication that went into getting them. When failure occurs, approach it with curiosity and a growth perspective, viewing it as a learning opportunity to build the culture.

5. Commit to continuous learning and development

- A leadership culture values learning. Leaders who prioritize growth and development foster an environment in which employees are encouraged to broaden their skills, knowledge, and perspectives. This dedication to learning ensures the organization's adaptability, innovation, and resilience.
- Invest in leadership development programs, training sessions, and possibilities for career advancement. Encourage your team members to gain new talents and share their knowledge with others. A focus on continual learning fosters a culture that is ready to tackle new problems and capitalize on new possibilities.

Culture in Action: Howard Schultz's Leadership

Howard Schultz, Starbucks' former CEO, is a prime example of The Law of Culture in action. When Schultz took over Starbucks, he aimed not just to construct a lucrative coffee company, but also to foster a culture of respect, honesty, and a common vision. Schultz's leadership style was defined by his emphasis on empowering staff, whom he referred to as "partners," as well as cultivating an environment of open communication and collaboration.

Schultz engaged his employees by offering thorough training, career progression possibilities, and benefits that indicated the company's dedication to their well-being. He also promoted open communication throughout the organization, soliciting views regularly and including employees in decision-making. Schultz created a corporation where leadership was a shared duty rather than a title.

Reflection: What kind of culture are you creating?

Ask yourself: Am I consciously shaping my organization's culture, or is it forming by default? What values and principles guide the way my team works, collaborates, and leads? Culture is not a static term; it is a dynamic force that leaders must cultivate and enhance.

Action Step:

This week, evaluate the culture of your organization or team. Determine one area in which you can model the behaviors and values you wish to see, and then take active actions to develop that component of your culture. Encourage your team to express their opinions on the type of culture they want to create together.

CHAPTER 11: THE LAW OF LEGACY

12

Chapter 12: The Law of Reproduction

Leaders Develop Leaders

"The function of leadership is to produce more leaders, not more followers." — Ralph Nader

The amount of followers one has does not define great leadership; rather, it is the leaders one creates. The Law of Reproduction emphasizes the fundamental idea that good leadership is not self-serving but creative. It is about putting seeds in others so that they can lead with confidence, character, and skill. The effectiveness with which a leader guides, mentors, and inspires those around them determines how successful they are.

Leadership, at its best, should leave a legacy that outlasts its founder. This is accomplished not by simply teaching individuals what to do, but by empowering them to become independent leaders. Leaders who believe in the Law of Reproduction understand that their job is not complete until they have prepared others to carry it forward.

CHAPTER 12: THE LAW OF REPRODUCTION

Why Leaders Must Develop Leaders

Developing leaders rather than followers causes a chain reaction that spreads a leader's impact beyond their immediate reach. Consider leadership development as the distinction between a leader who catches fish for a team and one who teaches the team how to fish. The latter method fosters long-term success and assures that when one leader leaves, the purpose continues to grow.

Principles for Developing Leaders

1. Identify and develop potential

- Effective leaders have a remarkable ability to identify potential in others. They understand that leadership qualities such as honesty, resilience, and empathy are not always visible, but they are worth developing. Identifying potential leaders begins with paying close attention to people who constantly show a desire to learn and contribute.
- Consider this: Are you actively hunting for those that show potential, or are you just concerned with results? Take the time to watch and promote those who exemplify the characteristics of future leaders.

2. Lead by example and set high standards

- Leaders who seek to emulate other leaders must model the concepts and values they wish to see. Leading by example entails exhibiting integrity, humility, and vision in all actions. When leaders set the standard through their behaviors, they leave a genuine template for others to follow.
- Consider your leadership style and the example you provide. What messages do your actions convey to your team? Ensure that your behaviors are consistent with the leadership culture you want to foster.

3. Mentor and empower with intentionality

- Mentoring is the intentional act of investing in others. It's about more than just giving counsel; it's about providing direction, accountability, and motivation. Leaders who reproduce leaders engage in regular mentorship, sharing their experiences as well as their future goals.
- Take a proactive attitude to mentoring. Develop true relationships with those you're mentoring, listen to their goals and concerns, and allow them to lead in modest but meaningful ways.

4. Offer real-world challenges and growth opportunities

- Leadership cannot be taught merely through theory. To genuinely replicate leaders, it is critical to present real-world problems that push budding leaders beyond their comfort zones. These difficulties promote resilience, confidence, and a practical grasp of leadership.
- Assign projects requiring critical thinking and decision-making. Allow people to feel the weight of leadership and support them as they negotiate these situations.

5. Develop a culture of feedback and reflection

- Leaders who prioritize others' development understand the importance of self-reflection and feedback. They foster a climate in which rising leaders are encouraged to analyze their actions, admit their faults, and adopt a philosophy of continual improvement.
- Create a culture in which feedback is normalized and valued. Encourage people you're developing to reflect on their experiences and offer constructive, concrete comments to help them progress.

CHAPTER 12: THE LAW OF REPRODUCTION

Leadership in Action: Nelson Mandela's Legacy

Nelson Mandela is an excellent example of the Law of Reproduction in action. During his presidency, Mandela's duty was not only to guide South Africa through a vital period of transformation but also to cultivate the next generation of leaders who would carry on that progress. Mandela recognized that the future of South Africa rested not on his influence, but on encouraging people to take ownership of the vision.

Mandela focused his efforts on mentoring and encouraging other activists, leaders, and people, building a culture of shared responsibility. His leadership style was based on humility, teamwork, and a firm conviction in the ability of others to lead effectively. Mandela's legacy continues as a result of his deliberate emphasis on leadership development, inspiring future generations.

Reflection: Are You Developing Leaders or Followers?

Ask yourself: Am I purposefully investing in others to become leaders, or am I simply creating dependents who rely on my guidance? True leadership broadens its impact by enabling others to lead with integrity and confidence.

Action Step:

Identify a team member with leadership potential. Schedule a time to talk about their goals, offer advice, and allow them to take on a new role or project. Commit to guiding them throughout the process and be intentional about their growth.

Strategies to Multiply Your Impact

"The greatest use of life is to spend it for something that will outlast it." — William James

The ultimate measure of a leader's performance is not just what they achieve personally, but also how their influence and vision spread to others. This notion is embodied in the Law of Multiplication. Exceptional leaders recognize that empowering others to lead and accomplish multiplies their success and impact, producing a ripple effect well beyond their immediate reach.

To increase your effect, actively shift your attention from simply leading others to empowering them to lead. It is about creating a culture in which every individual is empowered to contribute to the vision, accept responsibility, and lead within their sphere of influence. This chapter delves into crucial tactics for amplifying your leadership and inspiring others to generate long-term change.

1. Delegate with purpose, not just for relief.

- Many leaders fall into the trap of assigning responsibilities only to reduce their workload. However, really successful leaders delegate with purpose they regard delegation as a developing tool rather than an operational requirement. When assigning chores or projects, make it your goal to assist others to grow and build confidence in their talents.
- Identify areas where emerging leaders can take the lead and provide them with the necessary advice and resources to succeed. Delegating for developmental purposes moves your attention from efficiency to establishing a more capable and self-sustaining team.

2. Facilitate decision-making at all levels

- One of the most effective methods to broaden your impact is to foster an environment in which individuals feel empowered to make decisions. Leaders who centralize decision-making restrict their impact to their bandwidth. In contrast, individuals who transfer authority effectively establish several leadership touchpoints throughout their organization.
- Encourage individual decision-making to foster a trusting culture among

your team members. Set clear limits and limitations, but leave flexibility for innovation and ownership. This method not only broadens your effect but also promotes a sense of shared duty and accountability among your teammates.

3. Use Your Influence to Develop a Leadership Pipeline

- Every effective leader must be committed to identifying, developing, and equipping future leaders. Consider your leadership job as the start of a pipeline, not the end. Creating a leadership pipeline entails intentionally identifying potential leaders, coaching them, and providing them with the resources and opportunities they require to advance.
- Begin by recognizing those on your team who are eager to learn and contribute beyond their immediate responsibilities. Take the time to mentor them and allow them to advance into leadership positions. This not only prepares the future generation but also ensures that your vision and values are carried forward.

4. Establish a culture of accountability and ownership

- To multiply your effect, you must establish a sense of responsibility and accountability in the people you lead, not just delegate responsibilities. Leaders who promote accountability empower others to accept responsibility for their actions, decisions, and contributions.
- Encourage open communication, praise triumphs, and deal with failures constructively. When people feel accountable for their work and understand the value of their contributions, they become more committed to the mission and more willing to take on leadership roles.

5. Communicate the vision consistently and clearly

- Your ability to express your vision successfully determines how much impact you can have. Leaders who fail to communicate consistently create

opportunities for confusion and misalignment. However, by continuously sharing and reinforcing the vision, you can coordinate everyone's efforts and create a clear direction.
- Clarify your vision and values, then incorporate them into all conversations, meetings, and decisions. When people grasp the larger picture and how their contributions fit into the overarching objective, they are more likely to take the initiative and lead in their roles.

6. Prioritise Personal and Team Development

- The Law of Multiplication is based on personal and leadership development. Leaders must be dedicated to ongoing self-improvement and actively invest in the growth of their teams. This commitment entails more than simply technical training; it also includes instilling a growth mentality and creating chances for skill development, learning, and cooperation.
- Setting a good example can help to foster a culture of lifelong learning. Allocate resources for training, professional development, and mentorship programs that will help people attain their full potential.

Leadership in Action: Starbucks' Successful Leadership Culture

Starbucks has long been known not only for its coffee but also for its people-focused leadership culture. Former CEO Howard Schultz recognized that to properly build Starbucks, he needed to prioritize the development of leaders at all levels of the organization. Schultz was not only interested in expanding the firm; he was also interested in developing leaders.

Schultz fostered a culture of quality and integrity by giving store managers decision-making authority, promoting open communication, and prioritizing leadership development. This technique enabled Starbucks to swiftly expand while maintaining its mission and values, demonstrating the power of multiplying leadership influence.

CHAPTER 12: THE LAW OF REPRODUCTION

Reflection: Are you expanding or contracting your influence?

Question yourself: Am I actively multiplying my influence through others, or am I centralizing leadership and limiting my impact? Consider how you can increase your impact by educating, empowering, and mentoring others.

Action Step:

This week, pick one crucial area where you may delegate more efficiently and purposefully. Choose a task or project that you would normally handle and delegate it to a team member with specific instructions and the purpose of strengthening their skills. Assist, but enable them to lead the project to a conclusion.

V

Part 5: Mastering Leadership through Reflection and Practice

13

Chapter 13: The Law of Consistency

Stability Breeds Trust

"**Trust is built with consistency.**" — Lincoln Chafee

Leadership is based on trust, which is founded on stability. The Law of Stability emphasizes that people will only follow a leader they can trust one who is firm in their vision, constant in their conduct, and unshakeable in their convictions. Stability is not about being strict; it is about establishing a foundation of dependability and certainty so people may trust their leader's advice.

A leader's behaviors, decisions, and demeanor are predictable in a favorable way, which creates trust. People need to know that their leader is not reckless or unstable, but rather constant and dedicated to their cause. This consistency serves as the foundation for establishing and maintaining trust.

The Importance of Stability in Leadership

Stability is crucial for effective leadership, as it involves trust between the leader and followers. When people are unclear about their leader's actions or behavior, the relationship suffers, and their willingness to follow is reduced.

On the other side, leadership stability fosters confidence and a sense of security, allowing people to give their all.

Stability is displayed in three major areas: consistency in words and acts, emotional stability throughout crises, and adherence to ideals and values.

1. Consistency in words and actions

- Consistency is a fundamental feature of stability. Leaders who say one thing and conduct another instill uncertainty and distrust in their followers. To inspire confidence, a leader's words must be consistent with their actions, exhibiting integrity and dependability.
- Examine your communication and behavior: Are you delivering mixed signals, or are you following through on your promises? People respect leaders who "walk the talk" and regularly exemplify the ideals they promote.

2. Emotional Stability During Crisis

- In times of uncertainty or catastrophe, followers turn to their leaders for reassurance and direction. A leader who is emotionally steady under pressure sets the tone for the entire team. Emotional stability does not imply being emotion-free, but rather maintaining composure, lucidity, and resilience in difficult situations.
- Consider how you handle crises: Do you react hastily, or do you assess the issue and respond thoughtfully? Leaders who stay calm and controlled under pressure convey a feeling of stability to their followers.

3. Commitment to principles and values

- Stability also entails remaining unwavering in one's ideals and values. Leaders who frequently change their values to match the situation are perceived as untrustworthy. People must understand where their leader stands, especially when moral or ethical issues arise.

- Consider whether your decisions are governed by a clear set of values, or if you compromise those ideals when under duress. Leaders who stand steadfast on their values gain the trust and respect of the people they lead, even when those principles are questioned.

The Relationship Between Stability and Trust

Trust develops throughout time through a sequence of consistent, stable actions. Every time a leader follows through on their promises, keep calm under pressure, or stand solid in their ideals, they strengthen their credibility. Conversely, unpredictability and instability diminish trust, making it harder for individuals to believe in their leader's vision and decisions.

Leadership in action: Angela Merkel's steadfast leadership

Angela Merkel, Germany's former Chancellor, is a remarkable example of stable leadership. During her 16-year term, Merkel was noted for her calm demeanor, steady decision-making, and strong values. Throughout various crises, including the global financial crisis and the European migrant crisis, Merkel's consistent stance calmed both the German population and her European counterparts.

Merkel's capacity to remain calm in the face of hardship, together with her dedication to democratic values, gave her the reputation of a dependable and trustworthy leader. Her leadership proved the potential of stability to instill confidence and promote togetherness.

Reflection: Are You a Stabilising Presence?

Consider whether you are offering a steady and stable presence for those you lead, or if your actions and emotions are unpredictable. Stability is a choice that needs self-awareness, discipline, and adherence to beliefs.

Action Step:

This week, choose one area to improve your leadership stability. Whether it's being more consistent in your behaviors, regulating your emotions during stressful moments, or reiterating your basic principles, take deliberate measures to strengthen your stability and establish trust among your team.

Practicing What You Preach

"The most powerful leadership tool you have is your own personal example."
— John Wooden

Leadership without integrity is hollow. The Law of Integrity, "Practicing What You Preach," states that strong leaders do more than just talk about values; they embody them. They recognize that actions speak louder than words, and their behavior sets the tone for those who follow them. Integrity is more than just avoiding deception; it is also about living the principles you support with authenticity and consistency.

People will follow leaders who set an example rather than using hyperbole. If your words and actions are misaligned, your credibility and influence will suffer. In contrast, if you live up to the values you espouse, you inspire others to follow suit.

Why Integrity is Essential in Leadership

Leadership based on integrity fosters trust, which is the foundation of influence. When leaders practice what they preach, they display credibility, dependability, and authenticity. This alignment of words and actions promotes loyalty and respect, allowing leaders to effectively direct their people.

Without integrity, leaders may briefly command obedience through authority, but they will not inspire genuine loyalty or dedication. A lack of integrity breeds suspicion and skepticism, weakening the efficacy of even the best-intentioned leaders.

1. Aligning Words and Actions

- One of the most important components of integrity is to match your words with your deeds. Leaders who preach teamwork but act unilaterally, or who promote transparency while concealing critical facts, soon lose the trust of their colleagues. People want to see that their leader regularly demonstrates the principles they preach.
- Consider how your behaviors align with your declared values: Are you truly living up to what you require of others, or are there contradictions that damage your credibility? Remember that people tend to pay more attention to your actions than to your words.

2. Being honest and transparent

- Integrity necessitates honesty, even when the truth is unpleasant or inconvenient. Leaders who prioritize transparency, particularly in challenging situations, foster an environment of openness and trust. This includes being open and honest about mistakes, challenges, and decisions, as well as avoiding manipulation or deception in communication.
- Evaluate your communication style: Are you open and honest with your colleagues, or do you suppress facts to avoid awkward conversations? Embrace honesty, even when it is difficult, and you will get the respect of the people you supervise.

3. Accepting responsibility for your actions

- Leaders who practice what they preach are fully accountable for their actions and decisions. When mistakes are made, they do not shift blame or create excuses; instead, they accept responsibility and learn from their mistakes. This amount of accountability exhibits humility and honesty,

which inspires others to follow suit.
- Consider how you manage mistakes: do you accept responsibility, or do you divert blame? Accountability is more than just admitting mistakes; it is also about demonstrating a commitment to personal and professional development.

4. Demonstrating Consistency in Values

- Integrity compels leaders to maintain their values regardless of the circumstances. Situational integrity, in which principles vary depending on what is expedient or advantageous, undermines trustworthiness. Leaders must be firm on their ideals and make consistent decisions, even if they are unpopular or challenging.
- Consider this: Are your decisions governed by a clear set of basic ideals, or do you tailor your principles to the situation? True leaders are steadfast in their convictions and inspire others to do the same.

Leadership in Action: Mahatma Gandhi's Authenticity

Mahatma Gandhi, one of history's most famous leaders, exhibited the Law of Integrity by consistently living what he preached. Gandhi's idea of nonviolent resistance was more than a political technique; it was a profoundly held belief that he lived out in all aspects of his life. Gandhi's acts, both personal and public, were consistent with his values of simplicity, nonviolence, and self-discipline.

Gandhi's genuineness won the trust and loyalty of millions, allowing him to lead India's independence cause with moral authority. His life exemplifies the power of integrity in leadership, proving that when leaders live by their principles, people are inspired to follow with conviction.

Reflection: Do You Lead by Example?

Ask yourself: Am I truly practicing what I teach, or do my actions fall short of my words? Integrity necessitates continual self-reflection and a determination to align behavior with convictions.

Action Step:

This week, choose a principle or value that you espouse but may not always demonstrate. Make a conscious effort to match your behaviors with that value, and consider how this affects your team and your credibility as a leader.

14

Chapter 14: The Law of Priorities

Knowing What Must Come First

"The key is not to prioritize what's on your schedule, but to schedule your priorities." — Stephen Covey

Successful leaders don't try to achieve everything; instead, they prioritize what is most important. The Law of Priorities emphasizes the need to recognize and focus on the most crucial tasks, decisions, and initiatives with the biggest impact. Leadership is more than simply doing more; it is about doing what is necessary. Knowing what needs to come first enables leaders to maximize their performance and lead with purpose and clarity.

The Importance of Priority Setting in Leadership

Prioritization is more than simply a productivity tool; it is an essential leadership skill. Leaders who fail to prioritize stretch themselves too thin, becoming reactive rather than proactive. Leaders who understand what needs to be done first, on the other hand, may devote their time, energy, and resources to achieving their vision and goals.

Prioritization, however, is more than just chores; it is also about values and purpose. It entails making decisions based on what is consistent with the organization's mission and team goals, rather than just responding to external expectations or pressures.

1. Distinguish between Urgent and Important

- One of the most difficult aspects of prioritizing is deciding what is urgent and what is significant. Urgent jobs require immediate attention, but they are not usually the most meaningful or impactful in the long term. Important tasks, on the other hand, are consistent with your vision and goals, resulting in long-term success.
- Consider your daily activities: Are you always putting out fires, or are you actively focussing on what is genuinely important? Leaders who understand this distinction can focus on high-impact initiatives while handling pressing concerns without becoming overwhelmed.

2. Create a clear vision to guide your priorities

- Effective prioritization requires a strong understanding of your mission and values. Without a clear vision, it is difficult to discern what should come first. Leaders without clarity frequently prioritize based on convenience, external pressures, or short-term profits, resulting in misalignment and inefficiency.
- Ask yourself: Is my vision clear, and am I prioritizing tasks that bring me closer to it? Your vision should serve as a compass, directing your decisions and keeping you focused on what is truly important.

3. Prioritise High-Leverage Activities

- Leaders maximize their effect by focussing on high-leverage activities those that yield the greatest returns with the least amount of effort or time. Strategic planning, empowering others, and fostering innovation are common high-leverage activities that avoid becoming mired down in

minute details or administrative tasks.
- Consider your present workload: are you focusing on things that will have the most impact, or are you getting bogged down in low-leverage activities? Identify one or two high-impact initiatives that are aligned with your priorities and devote dedicated time to them every day.

4. Delegate Strategically to Maintain Focus

- Prioritization also entails understanding what you should not be doing. Leaders who strive to do everything for themselves lose sight of their actual priorities. Strategic delegation enables you to focus on your most important responsibilities while also empowering others to contribute to the purpose.
- Examine your workload: Are there any jobs that could be transferred to others, freeing you up to focus on what is most important? Delegation is more than just unloading work; it is also about encouraging your team to take ownership and thrive.

5. Review and reassess your priorities Regularly

- Prioritization is a continuous process rather than a single choice. Leaders must examine and reassess their priorities frequently to account for changing conditions, new information, and evolving ambitions. This flexibility guarantees that you stay on track with your vision and can change proactively.
- Set aside time each week to reflect: Are my present priorities still in line with my vision, or should I shift my focus? Regular reflection and adjustment help you be proactive rather than reactive in your leadership approach.

CHAPTER 14: THE LAW OF PRIORITIES

Leadership in Action: Steve Jobs and the Power of Focus.

When Steve Jobs returned to Apple in 1997, the company was battling to stay focused. Apple had a diverse portfolio of goods and programs, many of which were diluting the company's resources and clouding its vision. Jobs' first step as CEO was to eliminate 70% of Apple's product range, concentrating the company's resources on a few high-priority initiatives. This dramatic prioritization enabled Apple to focus on innovation and quality, resulting in the creation of iconic products such as the iMac, iPod, and iPhone.

Jobs recognized that knowing what came first was critical to Apple's rebirth. His drive to prioritization not only saved the corporation but also altered its future. Jobs' leadership proved that successful leaders focus tirelessly on what is most important and remove distractions that dilute their effectiveness.

Reflection: Are You Clear on Your Priorities?

Ask yourself: Am I clear on what has to come first, or am I spreading myself too thin across too many responsibilities? Prioritization necessitates clarity, discipline, and the willingness to say "no" to distractions.

Action Step:

This week, develop a list of your existing duties and obligations. Determine which one or two activities are most closely connected with your vision and will have the most influence on your objectives. Set aside time each day for these high-priority activities, and eliminate or assign chores that are not necessary.

How to Focus on What Matters Most

"Things which matter most must never be at the mercy of things which matter least." — Johann Wolfgang von Goethe

Effective leadership requires concentration focusing on what is genuinely important and letting go of distractions. The Law of Focus emphasizes the importance of devoting your energy and resources to the actions and goals that produce the best results. Leaders are frequently confronted with a bombardment of demands, difficulties, and opportunities; yet, the most successful leaders are those who understand what to prioritize and focus on.

The ability to focus on what is most important necessitates a clear vision, decision-making discipline, and the bravery to decline less important responsibilities. It is about aligning your behaviors with your objective and removing distractions that reduce your effectiveness.

The Dangers of Being Distracted

Distractions in leadership are not limited to external interruptions; they also include losing sight of your primary mission and purpose. Leaders who lack concentration are drawn in several directions, diluting their efforts and reducing their effect. When you're always reacting to little issues or new opportunities, you risk overlooking the important work that drives true development.

Being focused entails retaining a clear sense of direction in the face of external distractions. It entails understanding your objectives and focussing your resources and efforts on what will help you attain them.

1. Define What Matters Most

- The first step in focusing on what is important is to define it. Without a clear sense of priorities, you'll be tugged in numerous directions by conflicting demands. Leaders must develop a clear vision and priorities

to guide their decisions and activities.
- Consider: What are the fundamental aims and values that constitute my mission? What activities and duties are most directly related to those goals? Defining what is most important is the cornerstone for effective focus.

2. Make a clear plan and stick to it

- Once you've identified your priorities, you must devise a clear strategy to attain them. A well-thought-out strategy keeps you focused on what's most essential by offering a road map for your daily activities and decisions. However, a plan is only as effective as your willingness to keep to it.
- Consider your existing strategy. Do you have a clear plan that reflects your priorities, or are you improvising as you go? To keep on track, develop a structured strategy that represents your goal and review it on a frequent basis.

3. Reduce or delegate distractions

- To keep focused on what is most important, detect and remove distractions. Distractions can be either external, such as unneeded meetings or interruptions, or internal, such as self-doubt and procrastination. Leaders who recognize the importance of their time and energy make conscious attempts to maintain their focus.
- Consider your current distractions: Are there any tasks, habits, or interruptions that are taking you away from what is most important? Consider outsourcing non-essential chores or removing extraneous activities from your agenda.

4. Master the Art of Saying "No"

- Saying "no" can be difficult for leaders, especially when the opportunity

or request appears significant or urgent. However, focusing on what is most important demands the bravery to deny projects and obligations that do not correspond with your priorities. Leaders who say "yes" to everything eventually lose focus and become disorganized.
- Practice saying "no" politely but strongly. Are you willing to turn down requests or opportunities that do not correspond with your priorities, even if they are enticing or urgent? Remember that saying "no" to distractions is saying "yes" to your most essential goals.

5. Maintain your focus

- Focus necessitates accountability. Without responsibility, it is easy to deviate from your priorities and become reactive rather than proactive. Leaders who commit to regular self-reflection, feedback, and appraisal of their activities are more likely to remain focused on what is most important.
- Hold yourself accountable. Are you routinely analyzing your progress and realigning your actions to your priorities? Schedule regular check-ins to assess your focus and alter your strategy as necessary.

Leadership in Action: Warren Buffett's Strategy of Focus

Warren Buffett, one of history's most successful investors, is a master of focus. Buffett reportedly owes much of his success to his ability to focus on a few high-priority ventures while ignoring the others. He gave the following tip: "The difference between successful people and successful people is that successful people say no to almost everything."

Buffett's approach to focus is based on knowing what is most important investing in companies he understands and believes in and being disciplined enough to say no to distractions. His achievement demonstrates the importance of clear priorities and relentless focus.

Reflection: Are You Concentrated on What's Most Important?

Ask yourself: Am I clear about my priorities, and do I devote the majority of my time and attention to what is most important? Effective leadership necessitates ongoing attention to ensure that your priorities remain aligned with your objective.

Action Step:

This week, choose one significant objective or duty that is consistent with your priorities. Set aside focused, uninterrupted time each day to work towards that goal, and eliminate one typical distraction that draws you away from it. At the end of the week, consider how this emphasis has impacted your effectiveness.

15

Chapter 15: The Law of Sacrifice

Great Leadership Requires Giving Up to Go Up

"**You have to give up to go up.**" — John C. Maxwell

Leadership is about more than just obtaining control and attaining goals; it is also about making sacrifices. The Law of Sacrifice reminds us that leaders must frequently give up some conveniences, advantages, or smaller aims to attain something higher. It's a fundamental principle: you can't advance in leadership unless you give up something at your current position.

True leadership involves more than ambition; it necessitates the resolve to pay the price for advancement. This sacrifice is not always visible or appreciated. In truth, leaders' sacrifices are sometimes unrecognized and unappreciated, but they are critical to creating growth, success, and meaning.

The Myth of Perpetual Gain

One of the most popular myths about leadership is that it is all about acquiring power, responsibility, and recognition. However, exceptional leaders understand that each ascension necessitates a proportional sacrifice.

CHAPTER 15: THE LAW OF SACRIFICE

The higher you want to go, the more you must be prepared to give up.

Sacrifice in leadership can include giving up personal time, foregoing short-term pleasures for long-term impact, or standing back from specific activities to allow others to lead. It's about constantly asking yourself, "What must I let go of to achieve what's truly important?"

1. Giving Up Comfort for Growth

- Every leader reaches a point where staying comfortable equals becoming stagnant. Leaders who prioritize their comfort zone over growth pass up opportunities to expand, learn, and adapt. Growth frequently necessitates suffering discomfort, confronting problems head-on, and venturing into the unknown.
- Reflect on your journey: Are you sticking to comfort zones that are preventing you from accomplishing more? Accept discomfort as a necessary cost for growth.

2. Focussing on Team Success Over Personal Gain

- Great leaders prioritize their colleagues' needs before their aspirations. This involves putting your team's performance, progress, and well-being ahead of your recognition or advancement. Leaders who continuously make sacrifices for their teams build trust, loyalty, and unity.
- Ask yourself: Are you willing to prioritize your team's needs before your own? Servant leadership is defined by the willingness to sacrifice personal benefit for community accomplishment.

3. Giving Up Control to Empower Others

- One of the most difficult concessions for many leaders is losing power. Effective leaders recognize that to advance, they must let go of their urge to control every aspect or decision. Instead, they encourage others to take ownership, create, and lead on their terms.

- Examine your leadership style: are you willing to trust and empower people, even if it means giving up control? Giving up control not only encourages others' growth but also frees you up to focus on higher-level leadership tasks.

4. Giving Up Short-Term Pleasures for Long-Term Vision

- Sacrifice frequently involves giving up short-term joys or advantages in order to attain long-term success. Leaders with a strong vision are willing to defer gratification, avoid distractions, and remain focused on their ultimate goals. This concentration necessitates discipline and a realization that each sacrifice made today creates the groundwork for tomorrow's accomplishments.
- Consider your current actions: are you prioritizing instant benefits or staying focused on your long-term goals? Giving up short-term joys is necessary for long-term success.

5. Giving Up Ego to Serve Others

- Leadership is not about self-promotion; it is about helping others. To become a great leader, you must be prepared to put aside your ego and recognize that the objective and people you lead are more important than your pride. Humility is an effective form of sacrifice that fosters respect and trust.
- Ask yourself if you are willing to put your ego aside to help the people you lead. Sacrificing one's ego is an important step towards winning respect and motivating others to follow.

Leadership in Action: Nelson Mandela's Selfless Sacrifice.

Nelson Mandela is an excellent example of the Law of Sacrifice in action. Mandela spent nearly three decades in prison for his anti-apartheid activism. Despite the personal sacrifices he made—his freedom, his family life, and his youth—Mandela remained committed to attaining a bigger goal.

Mandela embraced the route of healing and unity after being released, rather than seeking revenge or personal benefit. His sacrifices helped to end apartheid and establish a democratic South Africa. Mandela's life exemplifies the power of sacrificing personal comfort and ambition for the greater good.

Reflection: Are You Willing to Make Sacrifices for Leadership?

Consider: What am I ready to give up to attain something greater? Leadership necessitates ongoing sacrifices of comfort, control, recognition, or short-term rewards. Consider what you may need to let go of to advance in your leadership development.

Action Step:

This week, identify one aspect of your leadership that you are overly attached to whether it is control, personal comfort, or recognition. Choose one little but significant sacrifice you can make to assist your team in success, growth, or progress. Consider the significance of this sacrifice, as well as the leadership development opportunities it provides for you and your teammates.

Learning When and How to Sacrifice

"The timing of your decision is just as important as the decision you make."
— John C. Maxwell

Leadership entails not just making the necessary sacrifices but also doing so at the appropriate time. Timing is critical in leadership. A well-intentioned sacrifice made too late can lose its meaning, but a sacrifice made too soon can leave you unprepared. Leaders must understand not only what to give up, but also when and how to let go for the best results.

This concept goes beyond simply ceding control or power. It also includes recognizing when to let go of a direction, idea, or even a role for your organization, team, or oneself to thrive.

The Essence of Strategic Sacrifice

Every leader will face situations in which difficult decisions must be taken. Strategic sacrifice is recognizing those moments, assessing the situation, and comprehending the broader consequences of your choices. It's about matching your actions to your goal while considering the long-term ramifications of what you give up.

Timing a sacrifice correctly helps you to divert resources, pivot to new opportunities, and demonstrate your dedication to a higher purpose or objective. However, knowing when to hang on and when to let go requires both insight and courage.

1. Understand the Bigger Picture

- The first step in mastering sacrifice is to see the larger picture. Effective leaders look beyond immediate concerns or challenges to consider the long-term consequences of their decisions. They evaluate their sacrifices not only in terms of immediate profits or losses but also in light of their overarching vision and objective.
- Consider: How does this decision fit into the overall mission? What long-term goals am I hoping to achieve? Understanding the wider perspective helps determine when a sacrifice is worthwhile.

2. Evaluate the cost-benefit ratio

- Leaders must consider the potential benefits and drawbacks of a sacrifice. This review looks at more than just financial costs and resources; it also considers the influence on morale, credibility, trust, and team dynamics. Great leaders understand when a sacrifice will result in major growth, progress, or stability, and when it will harm or set the team back.

- Consider the probable costs and rewards of this sacrifice. How will this decision affect the people I lead? Understanding the cost-benefit ratio eliminates rash judgments and ensures that your sacrifices are strategic and meaningful.

3. Recognise signs of change

- Change is unavoidable in leadership, and effective leaders understand when it is time to change direction or strategy. Recognizing the signals of change whether internal, such as team dynamics, or external, such as market conditions can help determine when compromises must be made to adapt and flourish.
- Reflect: Are there clear signals that a change is required? Is maintaining the existing method helping or harming progress? Recognizing the indicators of change enables leaders to pivot with confidence and purpose.

4. Letting Go so Others Can Grow

- Sacrificing control or specific responsibilities can be one of the most difficult yet critical decisions a leader can make. To promote other leaders within your organization or team, you must be willing to delegate work, authority, and even visibility in order to allow others to flourish and thrive. This sacrifice is not about losing power, but about increasing your impact.
- Consider whether you are willing to pull back and allow others to take the initiative. Allowing people to grow fosters an empowered and resilient culture among your team members.

5. Making a Decision with Precision

- Making sacrifices in leadership is a continuous process that demands smart timing. Leaders must be watchful, always monitoring the situation and adapting their actions to changing conditions. This necessitates humility, adaptability, and a willingness to acknowledge that what

worked yesterday may not work today.
- Consider: Is currently the appropriate moment to make this sacrifice, or should I wait? Leaders who make concessions too soon risk losing momentum, but those who wait too long may miss out on important opportunities.

Leadership in Action: Abraham Lincoln's Momentous Timing

Abraham Lincoln's decision to release the Emancipation Proclamation is a strong example of deliberate sacrifice executed with perfect timing. Though Lincoln personally despised slavery, he waited until the perfect moment to strike firmly. By waiting until the Union had won a substantial military victory at Antietam, Lincoln was able to issue the Proclamation from a position of strength, securing stronger political and popular support.

Lincoln's willingness to wait, despite the moral urgency of the situation, enabled him to have a lasting and profound impact at the appropriate time. His patience and strategic timing demonstrate the value of foregoing instant gratification for long-term success.

Reflection: Are You Willing to Sacrifice Strategically?

Ask yourself: Am I aware of when sacrifices must be made, and do I have the discipline to time them properly? Leadership requires a delicate balance of courage and patience, as well as the ability to recognize when it is time to let go for the larger good.

Action Step:

This week, identify one area of your leadership in which a sacrifice may be necessary. It might be discontinuing a project that no longer serves your objective, transferring responsibilities to empower others, or adjusting a strategy to adapt to changing circumstances. Consider the timing of this sacrifice and take a small, thoughtful move towards making it.

16

Chapter 16: The Law of Intuition

Leaders Read Situations and People

"Awareness precedes choice, and choice precedes change." — Robin Sharma

Great leaders have a keen understanding of both the situation and the people they lead. They are skilled in detecting the undercurrents of emotions, dynamics, and situations. This is not a passive ability; it is a deliberate practice that influences their decisions and actions. Leaders who master the skill of interpreting situations and people strengthen relationships, inspire trust, and effectively manage their teams through any problem.

This chapter emphasizes the need to cultivate awareness, develop emotional intelligence, and understand that effective leadership frequently begins with a clear vision.

1. Understanding situational dynamics

- Leadership is more than just problem-fixing; it is about predicting and negotiating complications before they occur. Effective leaders read the atmosphere of a situation, determining its urgency, underlying concerns,

and probable consequences. This situational awareness enables them to make informed decisions and take proactive steps.
- **Ask yourself:** What is going on behind the surface of this situation? Leaders who understand situational dynamics may recognize both problems and opportunities, allowing them to act precisely.

2. Listening Beyond the Words

- Reading people entails more than just understanding what they say; it is also about perceiving what they don't say. Leaders who carefully listen recognize body language, tone, and emotional clues. They understand that every word is a motivation, and every action is an aim.
- **Consider:** Are you sensitive to the unspoken messages in your interactions? Take the time to observe and listen, not only to what is said but also to what is felt and conveyed. This deeper level of listening fosters trust and improves partnerships.

3. Matching Leadership Style to the Situation

- Great leaders are flexible in their approach, understanding when to be assertive and when to be empathic. They read situations and tailor their leadership style to the needs of the time. A leader must provide clear direction at times, while also stepping back and empowering others.
- **Reflect:** Are you willing to change your style to meet the needs of your team and the situation? Adaptable leaders inspire confidence and resilience, demonstrating that they can handle any situation with ease.

4. Building Empathy and Emotional Intelligence

- Reading people is fundamentally about empathy. Leaders with high emotional intelligence can recognize when someone is struggling, disengaged, or needs encouragement. They may detect emotions beneath a confident facade or recognize frustration hidden behind quiet.

- **Consider:** How effectively do you understand and connect with the emotions of individuals you lead? Empathy is a valuable tool that helps leaders develop trust, manage issues, and motivate their staff.

5. Trusting Your Instincts and Intuition

- While facts and analysis are important, leaders must also trust their intuition. Intuition is typically the result of collected experience and the ability to see patterns that others may overlook. Great leaders understand when to trust their gut impulses, especially in confusing or high-pressure situations.
- **Consider this:** Do you trust your intuition in the face of uncertainty? Learning to reconcile rationality with intuition enables you to lead with confidence, especially in difficult situations.

Leadership in Action: Winston Churchill's Awareness in World War II

Winston Churchill's leadership during WWII is a powerful example of situational and personal awareness. As Prime Minister of Britain, Churchill grasped not only military dynamics but also British public morale. He understood the gravity of the situation and the emotions of his people, making speeches that were not just accurate but also genuinely motivating.

Churchill's ability to connect emotionally with his people while responding strategically to wartime circumstances exemplifies the importance of situational and personal awareness. He read the spirit of the country and responded decisively, inspiring his people to persevere at their darkest hour.

Reflection: Do you read situations and people?

Ask yourself: How well do you comprehend the dynamics around you and the feelings of people you lead? Leadership is more than just making decisions; it is about seeing clearly and acting intelligently.

Action Step:

This week, develop situational and personal awareness in your leadership. Pay special attention to the unspoken dynamics at a critical meeting or interaction. Consider the mood, body language, and underlying tensions. Consider how your awareness influences your decisions and relationships, and take deliberate steps to improve your understanding of the people you manage.

Developing an Insightful Leadership Approach

"Leadership is not about titles, positions, or flowcharts. It is about one life influencing another." — John C. Maxwell

Great leaders have a clear vision and a thorough awareness of the world around them. This kind of understanding does not occur by chance; it is the consequence of deliberate observation, contemplation, and learning. Insightful leaders recognize trends, anticipate obstacles, and make decisions that are consistent with their mission and values. They are self-aware and focused on their team, leading with wisdom and forethought.

1. Developing the Habit of Reflection

- Insightful leaders do more than respond; they also reflect. They take the time to step back and examine circumstances, determining not just what is occurring but also why it is happening. Reflection enables them to discover fresh insights, learn from past experiences, and adapt their strategies accordingly.
- **Ask yourself:** Am I making time for regular reflection? Take time each week to reflect on important decisions, interactions, and obstacles. What did you learn, and how will you apply it in the future?

2. Seeking to Understand, Not Just Leading

1. Leadership entails both knowing and directing others. Insightful leaders are curious about their team's motivations, challenges, and goals. They ask insightful questions and pay close attention to what others have to say.

- Consider whether you want to understand the people you lead, or if you are only concerned with directing them. Make it a point to listen actively and offer open-ended questions to gain new perspectives and insights.

3. Recognising patterns and connecting dots

- One of the distinguishing characteristics of insightful leadership is the capacity to recognize patterns and link seemingly unrelated dots. This competence enables leaders to predict obstacles, identify opportunities, and respond clearly. Insightful leaders see beyond individual pieces to understand the overall picture.
- **Consider:** Are you looking beyond current issues to uncover repeating patterns? Consider how minor issues or behaviors can indicate broader trends or root reasons.

4. Being self-aware and honest

- Insightful leaders are extremely self-aware. They recognize their talents, limitations, and biases, and they are willing to face hard realities about themselves. Self-awareness enables individuals to lead truly and make decisions that reflect their basic convictions.
- **Ask yourself:** How well do I understand myself as a leader? Take some time to evaluate your skills, places for improvement, and blind spots. Self-awareness is the foundation of intelligent leadership; it allows you to lead with honesty and humility.

5. Accepting Complexity with Confidence

- Leadership frequently requires handling complex, ambiguous situations. Insightful leaders embrace complexity instead of avoiding it. They recognize the difficulties and contradictions of leadership and respond with flexibility and grace.
- **Consider:** Are you comfortable dealing with complexity, or do you avoid uncertain situations? Practice accepting the ambiguity of leadership with confidence, believing in your ability to find clarity amid chaos.

Leadership in Action: Nelson Mandela's Thoughtful Approach to Unity

Nelson Mandela's Leadership in Post-Apartheid South Africa is an excellent example of an insightful strategy. Mandela recognized that to govern a highly divided country, he had to prioritise unity and reconciliation over vengeance or retribution. He recognized the patterns of division and misery in his society and opted to lead with empathy, understanding, and vision.

Mandela's wisdom allowed him to guide South Africa towards healing, paving the way forward despite profound wounds and institutional hurdles. His leadership exemplifies the ability of insight to influence a nation and inspire future generations.

Reflection: Are You Developing an Insightful Leadership Approach?

Consider whether you are actively attempting to gain a better understanding of situations, others, and yourself. Insightful leadership isn't about having all the answers; it's about being open to seeing the bigger picture and responding with wisdom and humility.

Action Step:

Develop your leadership insights this week. Set aside time for introspection, try to understand your team's motives, and observe patterns in your organization. Determine one area where increased information could lead to a more considered and productive decision, and then act on your new knowledge.

Chapter 17: The Law of Momentum

The Power of Positive Momentum in Leadership

"**Momentum breeds motivation, and motivation creates more momentum.**" — John C. Maxwell

Momentum is one of the most potent elements in leadership. It's the unseen power that pulls teams ahead, turns obstacles into opportunities, and converts tiny victories into long-term success. Leaders who appreciate the value of positive momentum focus not just on achieving goals, but also on creating and maintaining momentum to keep progress moving forward.

1. Building Momentum with Small Wins

- Momentum does not begin with spectacular triumphs; it begins with little, persistent victories. Leaders who understand this focus on setting a succession of reachable goals that gradually instill confidence, energy, and passion in their teams. Each success, no matter how modest, encourages a sense of accomplishment and faith in the larger purpose.
- **Ask yourself:** Are you enjoying and acknowledging minor victories

along the way? Recognizing these accomplishments fosters a culture of positivity and growth, motivating your team to keep moving forward.

2. Lead with energy and enthusiasm

- Momentum is powered by energy, and as a leader, your excitement is infectious. When leaders show passion, commitment, and belief in their cause, individuals around them are inspired to match their intensity. Leaders who continually bring positivity and drive to their jobs foster an environment in which momentum flourishes.
- Consider whether you are leading with the enthusiasm you want your team to embody. Your attitude and excitement set the tone for the team's morale and readiness to work through difficulties.

3. Staying Focused Despite Distractions

- Distractions, setbacks, and competing priorities can all quickly deplete momentum. Great leaders maintain momentum by remaining focused on their objectives and encouraging their teams to do the same. They prioritize what is most important, driving their team with clarity and direction.
- **Reflect:** Are you allowing distractions to impede your team's progress? Maintain discipline in your concentration and assist your team in aligning their efforts with the overarching purpose to keep moving forward.

4. Turning Challenges into Catalysts

- Challenges have the potential to derail or strengthen momentum. Setbacks, in the eyes of insightful leaders, are chances for growth and innovation. They urge their staff to confront problems with resilience and a solution-oriented mindset, transforming challenges into moments of breakthrough.
- **Ask yourself:** Are you approaching issues with a momentum-building

mindset? Reframe challenges as opportunities for progress, and motivate your team to overcome setbacks with tenacity.

5. Maintaining Momentum with Consistent Action

- Leadership momentum is not sustained by sporadic efforts; it is built on consistency. Leaders who maintain momentum prioritize consistent action, progress checks, and ongoing improvement. They recognize that consistency fosters trust, strengthens commitment, and drives the team forward.
- Consider whether you and your team are taking constant action toward your goals. Regular, intentional progress keeps momentum going, even when the path is difficult.

Leadership in Action: Martin Luther King Jr.'s Momentum for Change.

Dr. Martin Luther King Jr.'s leadership in the Civil Rights Movement shows the importance of momentum in accomplishing long-term change. King realized that momentum would be built over time by a series of persistent activities, organized efforts, and incremental successes. From the Montgomery Bus Boycott to the March on Washington, he led with unflinching energy, emotion, and a clear commitment to the cause of equality.

King's ability to generate and sustain momentum sparked a movement, inspiring millions to join the cause and ultimately changing the course of history. His leadership is a striking reminder that positive momentum, once established, can become an unstoppable force for change.

Reflection: Are you creating and sustaining positive momentum?

Ask yourself if you are purposefully building and keeping momentum in your leadership. Positive momentum is a force multiplier—it accelerates development, fosters belief, and creates long-term influence.

Action Step:

This week, focus on creating good momentum within your team. Identify one modest victory you can assist your team achieve and celebrate it together. Take conscious measures to lead with energy and excitement, and commit to staying focused on what is most important. Consistent action, positive energy, and resilience will help you gain momentum.

How to Start and Sustain Momentum in a Team

"Momentum is the great exaggerator. It makes leaders look better than they are, and it makes problems seem smaller than they are." — John C. Maxwell

Momentum is the unseen power that propels regular teams into great ones. It's the constant motivation that keeps everyone going forward, collaborating, and aiming for a single objective. The most effective leaders recognize that gaining momentum is more than just pushing harder; it is also about providing the conditions for energy and development to thrive.

1. Set clear and achievable goals

- Clarity is the first step towards building momentum. When teams grasp their objectives and see a clear route forward, they are inspired to act. However, these objectives must be achievable. Setting overly ambitious goals can lead to frustration and stagnation, whereas attainable goals boost confidence and motivation.
- Ask yourself if your team's goals are clear, detailed, and achievable. Begin by clearly outlining short-term objectives that are consistent with the overall mission. When your team meets these tiny objectives, their belief in the mission rises, as does their momentum.

2. Celebrate little wins to boost confidence

- Momentum builds on progress. Each win, no matter how minor, boosts a team's confidence and vitality. Celebrating these victories is critical because it supports the team's sense that their efforts are worthwhile and that they can succeed.
- Consider whether you are taking the time to celebrate little accomplishments with your team. Recognize and celebrate their success, and use these opportunities to instill a sense of accomplishment and solidarity.

3. Establish a culture of positivity and purpose

- A pleasant environment provides fertile ground for momentum. Leaders who inspire optimism, encourage others, and emphasize the team's goal foster an environment in which development feels natural and attainable. This does not imply disregarding obstacles, but rather keeping a positive and solution-oriented mindset.
- **Consider:** Are you cultivating a culture of positivity and shared purpose within your team? Encourage open communication, mutual support, and maintaining the team's focus on the broader picture. A positive culture provides a solid foundation for long-term progress.

4. Maintain consistent communication

- Miscommunication and a lack of direction can easily break momentum. Leaders who maintain momentum communicate consistently and effectively. They provide regular updates, comments, and encouragement to keep everyone aligned and motivated.
- **Consider this:** Are you consistently talking with your staff to keep them focused and informed? Make it a practice to check in frequently, provide clear guidance, and listen to the team's needs and concerns. Clear communication fosters a sense of unity and collaborative progress.

5. Address challenges proactively

- Obstacles and failures are unavoidable, but how a leader responds makes all the difference. Insightful leaders address issues proactively, preventing them from derailing the team's progress. They do not wait for problems to escalate; instead, they address them head-on with solutions.
- **Consider this:** Are you taking aggressive steps to address team challenges? Stay attentive for any roadblocks and respond swiftly to provide assistance, guidance, or course corrections as needed. Leaders who approach obstacles with confidence maintain their team's momentum.

6. Lead with energy and vision

- Momentum requires energy, and as a leader, yours is contagious. Leaders who lead with energy and a compelling vision inspire their teams to stay motivated and committed. Leaders who are passionate about their missions energize others and create a positive ripple effect of activity.
- **Consider:** Do you lead with enthusiasm and a clear vision? Consistently express your enthusiasm and dedication to the team's objectives. Your enthusiasm and belief in the purpose will motivate others to do their best.

Leadership in Action: Steve Jobs' Vision-Driven Momentum at Apple.

Steve Jobs' leadership at Apple is an excellent example of building and maintaining momentum via vision and drive. Jobs saw that for Apple to survive, it required not only inventive goods but also a strong sense of purpose. His enthusiasm for simplicity and quality was contagious, inspiring his team to push the envelope and accomplish what was impossible.

Jobs also understood the need to celebrate accomplishments and maintain regular communication. By consistently communicating his ideas and showing confidence in his team's ability, he fostered momentum. His leadership enabled Apple to revolutionize the technology industry and achieve global success.

Reflection: Do You Start and Maintain Momentum in Your Team?

Ask yourself if you are actively providing the circumstances for momentum to grow inside your team. Building and maintaining momentum is not about pushing harder; rather, it is about fostering the energy, clarity, and positivity that fuels continual growth.

Action Step:

This week, focus on creating and maintaining momentum within your team. Set a specific, attainable goal, appreciate little victories, and proactively handle any potential problems. Lead with enthusiasm, communicate consistently, and foster a good atmosphere that encourages action. Remember that momentum multiplies when leaders deliberately foster it.

18

Chapter 18: The Law of Buy-In

Gaining Commitment and Ownership

"People don't commit to what you tell them to do; they commit to what they believe in." — John C. Maxwell

Leadership is more than just convincing people to follow; it's also about encouraging them to commit and take responsibility for their jobs. When people feel personally invested in a project, they transition from mere compliance to genuine dedication. They don't just execute things; they care about the outcome and put forth their best efforts.

1. communicate the mission and purpose

- People commit when they believe in the mission. Leaders must be able to convey not only what has to be done, but why it is important. When people realize the importance of their job and how it relates to a bigger mission, they are more motivated to spend their time and abilities.
- **Ask yourself:** Are you effectively explaining the aim of your team's work? Go beyond the directions and convey the significance and value of your mission. A clear "why" inspires emotional connection and true

dedication.

2. Involve the Team in Decision-Making

- Ownership grows when people feel they have a voice in the decisions that affect their work. Leaders who actively seek input and involve their team in key decisions build trust and encourage buy-in. People are far more likely to commit to something they helped shape.
- **Consider:** Are you giving your staff opportunities to give ideas and perspectives? Encourage open communication and respect for other points of view. A collaborative approach fosters commitment and team cohesion.

3. Empower People with Responsibility

- Ownership grows when leaders encourage their team members to accept responsibility for their roles and outcomes. Trusting your staff to make decisions and delegating authority promotes a sense of ownership. When people feel trusted and capable, they rise to the situation and are proud of their contributions.
- **Reflect:** Are you giving your team members the autonomy they require to take ownership? Avoid micromanaging and instead, provide direction and assistance while allowing them to take ownership of their responsibilities.

4. Encourage Accountability with Support

- True ownership necessitates accountability. Leaders should foster an environment in which accountability is viewed as a tool for progress rather than a punishment. This entails holding people accountable for their promises while also giving them the assistance and tools they require to achieve.
- Consider whether you're encouraging accountability positively and helpfully. Balance expectations with encouragement, and recognize that

accountability is a shared responsibility for leaders and their teams.

5. Develop a sense of belonging and team identity

- People's commitment grows deeper when they have a genuine connection to their team. Leaders who foster a sense of belonging and identity help their teams perceive themselves as essential components of a bigger whole. This sense of belonging and pride in the team encourages loyalty and dedication.
- Consider whether you actively promote a sense of belonging and team identity. Celebrate team accomplishments, establish traditions, and instill the belief that each individual's contribution is valuable and meaningful.

Leadership in action: Southwest Airlines' ownership culture under Herb Kelleher

Herb Kelleher, Southwest Airlines' co-founder, recognized that garnering commitment and ownership from his employees was critical to building a healthy business culture. Kelleher prioritized creating a sense of family and shared purpose inside the organization, fostering open communication, and empowering staff to make decisions that benefit consumers.

Kelleher's leadership philosophy was straightforward: "The business of business is people." By treating people with trust and respect, he created a culture in which everyone felt a strong sense of ownership and pride in their job. This approach allowed Southwest Airlines to sustain high levels of customer satisfaction and loyalty, which were fuelled by a workforce that was committed to the company's mission.

Reflection: Are You Gaining Team Commitment and Ownership?

Consider whether you're inspiring genuine dedication and developing a sense of ownership among your team members. Trust, communication, and a shared sense of purpose are the foundations of ownership; it is about meaning rather than chores.

Action Step:

This week, prioritize gaining commitment and ownership from your team. Begin by clearly articulating the reason for your team's goals. Create a collaborative environment, assign responsibility to your team, and promote positive accountability. Reinforce a sense of belonging by acknowledging and celebrating each team member's accomplishments. Remember that true ownership is not forced; it is inspired.

Earning People's Trust and Support

"Trust is the glue of life. It's the most essential ingredient in effective communication. It's the foundational principle that holds all relationships." — Stephen Covey

Leadership is based on trust. When people believe in their leader, they are willing to follow, support, and invest in the common mission. However, trust is not given freely; it must be earned through constant conduct, integrity, and real concern for the people you lead. Leaders who prioritize trust foster strong relationships that inspire commitment, collaboration, and perseverance, even in the face of adversity.

1. Lead with integrity and authenticity

CHAPTER 18: THE LAW OF BUY-IN

- Integrity is the foundation of trust. People are naturally drawn to leaders who are authentic, truthful, and unwavering in their commitment to doing the right thing. Authenticity and honesty build trust, allowing others to regard you as a dependable and moral leader.
- Consider whether you constantly demonstrate integrity and honesty in your behaviors and decisions. Be forthright about your intentions and communicate clearly. When others see that you lead with authenticity, trust develops organically.

2. Demonstrate consistency in actions and words

- People believe in leaders who are reliable and consistent. If your words match your actions, you demonstrate that you are trustworthy and devoted to what you say. Consistency does not imply perfection; rather, it is being present in all contexts.
- Consider whether your actions reflect your statements. Strive to lead in a constant, predictable, and reliable manner. Inconsistencies can destroy trust and raise doubt, so strive to be the same leader in good times and bad.

3. Listen actively and empathically

- Genuinely listening is one of the most effective methods to create trust. Everyone wants to be heard, understood, and valued. Leaders who actively and empathetically listen display a genuine interest in their team's viewpoints, difficulties, and ideas. This approach strengthens trust and encourages open communication.
- **Reflect:** Are you listening to your team, or are you simply hearing them? Take the time to listen without interrupting, recognize their problems, and answer with empathy. People feel respected and valued when they know they have been heard.

4. Be willing to admit mistakes and learn from them

- No leader is perfect, and claiming to be infallible can swiftly undermine trust. Admitting mistakes, accepting inadequacies, and demonstrating a willingness to improve increases credibility and humility. Leaders who are open about their mistakes earn respect and build trust with their teams.
- **Ask yourself:** Are you willing to confess your mistakes? Accept vulnerability, admit your mistakes, and show a willingness to learn and improve. Humility in leadership fosters trust and loyalty.

5. Prioritise the well-being of your team

- People trust leaders who truly care about them—not just as employees, but as individuals. Prioritizing your team's well-being, both professionally and personally, fosters trust and shows that you appreciate them beyond their contributions to the mission.
- **Consider:** Do you genuinely care about your team's well-being? Make it a point to check in with them, offer assistance, and be there in times of need. When others feel valued, they are more likely to trust and support you in return.

Leadership in action: Oprah Winfrey: Empathy and Authenticity

Oprah Winfrey's journey from a difficult childhood to becoming a global media icon exemplifies the importance of empathy and authenticity in leadership. Oprah's success stems not only from her economic acumen but also from her ability to connect with people on a deep emotional level. She earned millions of people's trust and support by being honest about her own experiences, listening empathetically, and acting with integrity consistently.

Oprah's leadership style emphasized that by leading with authenticity, empathy, and unflinching integrity, you build a solid foundation of trust. Her audience and employees both perceived her as someone who actually cared, and that trust was critical to her long-term influence and success.

CHAPTER 18: THE LAW OF BUY-IN

Reflection: Are You Gaining People's Trust and Support?

Ask yourself: Am I continuously earning trust via my conduct, integrity, and concern for others? Trust is a constant process that involves intention and effort.

Action Step:

This week, prioritize building trust with your team. Commit to acting consistently and communicating transparently. Engage in active listening and show empathy in your relationships. Accept responsibility for your mistakes and put your team's well-being first. Remember that trust is earned day by day, one authentic action at a time.

19

Chapter 19: The Law of the Inner Circle

Leaders' Strength Is Their Inner Circle

"A leader's potential is determined by those closest to them." — John C. Maxwell

No leader succeeds alone. Great leaders recognize that their influence, vision, and success are inextricably linked to the strength of their inner circle. This group includes trusted advisors, significant team members, and close collaborators who contribute their knowledge, insight, and support. A leader's strength is determined not just by their abilities, but also by the collective power of people with whom they choose to surround themselves.

1. Choose people who can complement your strengths and compensate for your weaknesses.

- An effective inner circle is not comprised of clones of the leader. Instead, it should include people with a variety of abilities, viewpoints, and skills. These individuals fill in the gaps, challenge preconceptions, and offer unique skills. Leaders who actively seek out complimentary team members increase their effectiveness.

- Consider whether you've chosen folks whose distinctive abilities and perspectives will boost your leadership. Recognize your limitations and form a team to compensate for them. The goal is to build a diverse and dynamic group that will strengthen both you and the organization.

2. Promote Deep Trust and Loyalty Within Your Circle

- The inner circle is more than simply a team; it is a close-knit community united by mutual trust and loyalty. Leaders must prioritize developing these relationships through transparency, consistency, and open communication. Trust enables members to share honest criticism, express concerns, and assist one another during difficult times.
- **Consider:** Are you actively building trust within your close circle? Create an environment in which honesty is valued and disagreements may be discussed freely without fear of being judged. Strong trust provides a firm foundation for collaboration and mutual growth.

3. Empower and develop your Inner Circle members

- A leader's success is determined by her or his capacity to empower and uplift others around them. Leaders who invest in the growth and development of their inner circle build a powerful, self-sustaining group capable of doing great things. This includes not only mentoring and coaching but also empowering them to lead in their areas of competence.
- **Reflect:** Do you help your inner circle members reach their full potential? Create opportunities for advancement, encourage people to take on difficulties, and provide direction as needed. Leaders who inspire people form a powerful and motivated inner circle.

4. Encourage open discussion and honest feedback

- An effective inner circle is not only a gang of 'yes-men.' Leaders should encourage open communication and honest feedback among their inner

circle. Constructive criticism and open communication are essential for personal and community development.
- Ask yourself if you are fostering an environment in which your inner circle feels comfortable sharing feedback. Make it apparent that their input is valued, and be willing to change direction if required. Accept the strength that comes from multiple perspectives and honest feedback.

5. Acknowledge and celebrate the accomplishments of your inner circle

- Building a solid inner circle is more than just strategy; it's about connection. Leaders who take the time to acknowledge and appreciate their inner circle's accomplishments foster a sense of shared pride and accomplishment. This not only develops ties but also encourages the group to keep striving for success.
- **Consider:** Do you recognize and appreciate your inner circle's accomplishments? Recognize their efforts, share successes together, and express gratitude for their devotion and dedication. Shared celebrations strengthen ties and increase devotion to the purpose.

Leadership in Action: Winston Churchill's Inner Circle. During World War II.

During World War II, Winston Churchill's inner circle of loyal advisors aided his leadership significantly. Churchill realized he couldn't lead the country through its most difficult era alone. He surrounded himself with people who were not only skilled but also willing to question his ideas and offer open advice.

Churchill appreciated multiple opinions and relied on his inner circle to provide strategic insights and help him make judgments. The trust and loyalty he fostered among this group were critical to their ability to collaborate successfully, even under extreme strain. By embracing and strengthening his inner circle, Churchill was able to inspire and lead a nation at one of its darkest periods.

CHAPTER 19: THE LAW OF THE INNER CIRCLE

Reflection: Are you creating a strong inner circle?

Ask yourself if you are purposefully developing an inner circle that strengthens your leadership. Your inner circle is more than simply a reflection of your current leadership; it is a critical aspect of your long-term success.

Action Step:

This week, assess the effectiveness and dynamics of your inner group. Identify areas where you can broaden your abilities and ideas, and then focus on building trust within the group. Empower your inner circle members, promote open communication, and acknowledge their accomplishments. Remember that your leadership potential is defined by those closest to you—make sensible decisions, invest fully, and lead collaboratively.

Building a Team of Trusted Advisors

"Surround yourself with the best people you can find, delegate authority, and don't interfere." — Ronald Reagan

No leader can prosper without reliable advisors. They serve as a sounding board, guiding light, and a reality check for the leader. The most effective leaders recognize that success cannot be achieved alone; it requires a team of experienced, smart, and supportive advisors who provide insight, encouragement, and perspective.

1. Find advisors with diverse strengths and experiences.

- Trusted advisors deliver more than simply knowledge; they provide a variety of perspectives, experiences, and abilities. Leaders must be deliberate in picking advisors that complement their skills and provide comprehensive views. Leaders get a better grasp of situations and can

approach problems with greater creativity and foresight by bringing together people from various backgrounds and experiences.
- Consider whether you are hiring advisors who bring a diverse range of perspectives and experiences to the table. Don't only hunt for people who agree with you; instead, seek out those who can challenge your assumptions and help you improve.

2. Develop relationships based on mutual respect and trust

- Mutual trust and respect are essential components of every adviser engagement. Leaders must build relationships in which advisers feel valued and respected, as well as a shared commitment to the leader's performance and the goals of the organization. This mutual trust fosters honest feedback and provides a safe environment for meaningful talks.
- Consider whether you are cultivating connections with your advisors based on trust and mutual respect. Spend time getting to know them personally, learning their principles, and establishing a solid basis of mutual respect and understanding.

3. Be Open to Feedback, Even When It's Hard to Hear

- Effective advisors provide leaders with the information they need, not simply what they want to hear. Leaders must be willing to receive candid, sometimes tough input from their advisors. This openness necessitates humility and a willingness to prioritize the purpose over personal ego.
- **Reflect:** Are you willing to accept feedback with an open mind? Encourage your advisors to talk freely and be willing to listen, even if their thoughts contradict yours.

4. Empower your advisors to lead in their areas of expertise

- Trust requires reciprocation. Leaders must be willing to allow their advisors to take the initiative in their areas of competence. Leaders

demonstrate their appreciation for their advisers' contributions and faith in their judgment by delegating authority and allowing them to give their ideas.
- Ask yourself if you are empowering your advisors to take on leadership responsibilities. Delegate duties and empower your advisers to lead in their areas of expertise. When they feel trusted and empowered, they become even more committed to your common objective.

5. Maintain a Regular and Open Line of Communication

- The success of an advisory team is dependent on clear and regular communication. Leaders must schedule regular check-ins, address difficulties, and explore solutions with their advisors. Open communication promotes collaboration and keeps everyone aligned and informed.
- Consider whether you maintain open and constant communication with your advisors. Set up regular meetings or touchpoints to address significant issues, share updates, and solicit feedback. Maintain open lines of communication to build trust and teamwork.

Leadership in action: Abraham Lincoln's "Team of Rivals"

Abraham Lincoln's leadership throughout the Civil War is a great example of assembling a trustworthy team of advisors. Despite enormous hurdles, Lincoln surrounded himself with a collection of people, many of whom were previous political adversaries, who provided a variety of ideas and skills to his administration. Lincoln recognized that having advisors who would challenge his views was critical to making sound decisions and guiding the country through a crisis.

Lincoln's ability to listen to opposing ideas, along with his devotion to empowering his advisors, generated a powerful dynamic that benefited both his leadership and the nation as a whole. His "team of rivals" demonstrated the importance of assembling a group of trusted advisors who could offer candid feedback, strategic advice, and unshakeable support.

Reflection: Are You Building a Trusted Advisors Team?

Consider: Am I intentionally assembling a team of trusted advisors to challenge, support, and strengthen my leadership? Your advisers are more than just consultants; they are valuable partners in your leadership development.

Action Step:

This week, prioritize developing and cultivating your valued advisors. Evaluate the qualities and experiences of those closest to you, and seek out new viewpoints. Commit to keeping open communication and accepting feedback with humility. Empower your advisers to take the lead in their areas of expertise, and foster relationships built on mutual trust and respect. Remember, strong leaders surround themselves with the best people and seek their advice.

20

Chapter 20: The Law of Influence Multiplication

Multiplying Influence through Collaboration

"If you want to go fast, go alone. If you want to go far, go together."
— African Proverb

Great leaders recognize that teamwork magnifies their effect. Leadership is more than just guiding others; it is about inspiring, empowering, and working with them to create something better than any individual could accomplish alone. True influence does not come from exercising control; it comes from collaborating with others to achieve mutual success. When leaders prioritize collaboration, they increase their influence and cause a ripple effect that goes well beyond their efforts.

1. Embrace the Strength of Diverse Perspectives

- Collaboration flourishes when leaders actively seek out and value varied viewpoints. Leaders promote innovation, creativity, and well-rounded decision-making by bringing together team members from various back-

grounds, experiences, and perspectives. A collaborative workplace that appreciates diversity produces more effective solutions and impactful results.
- **Consider this:** Do you purposefully include various viewpoints in your collaborations? Go beyond the apparent options and actively engage people who can bring new ideas and perspectives to the table.

2. Move from Control to Empowerment

- A leader who focuses on managing every facet of a project restricts the team's potential and stifles growth. Collaborative leaders, on the other hand, empower their teams by distributing responsibility, promoting autonomy, and allowing individuals to take ownership of their work. When team members feel trusted and empowered, they are more committed to the collaboration's success.
- **Consider:** Are you willing to relinquish control and empower others? Adopt a leadership style that promotes autonomy, and allows your team to offer their unique skills and ideas.

3. Promote a culture of open communication and mutual respect

- Collaboration necessitates an environment in which team members are comfortable sharing their views, ideas, and feedback. Leaders must foster an environment of open communication and mutual respect, in which everyone's opinion is appreciated and honest interactions are encouraged. This strategy not only improves the team but also fosters trust and loyalty.
- **Reflect:** Are you encouraging open communication among your team members? Create regular opportunities for collaboration, encourage honest input, and actively listen to what others are saying.

4. Lead with a collaborative mindset

- Leaders who prioritize cooperation approach their positions from a

partnership rather than a hierarchical perspective. They perceive themselves as facilitators rather than team leaders, guiding, inspiring, and supporting others. By adopting a collaborative mentality, leaders foster an inclusive environment in which everyone feels appreciated and driven to contribute.
- Do you see leadership as a partnership rather than a position of authority? Change your perspective from being the team's focal point to a catalyst for group success.

5. Recognise and celebrate shared achievements

- When collaboration results in success, it's critical to acknowledge and honor the accomplishments of all team members. Leaders who recognize and appreciate their team's efforts foster a positive and stimulating environment. Celebrating shared accomplishments not only raises morale but also stresses the importance of working together to achieve common objectives.
- **Consider:** Do you recognize your team's joint achievements? Take the time to celebrate accomplishments and express gratitude to each team member. Remember that collaboration is an ongoing process, and each step forward deserves to be acknowledged.

Leadership in Action: The Effectiveness of Collaborative Leadership in Apollo 11

The success of the Apollo 11 mission, which landed the first humans on the moon, demonstrates the value of collaborative leadership. While Neil Armstrong, Buzz Aldrin, and Michael Collins are frequently honored, the mission's accomplishment was made possible by the efforts of thousands of workers from other disciplines, including engineers, scientists, mathematicians, and support personnel.

NASA's leaders recognized that their influence and impact could only be magnified by the combined efforts of a devoted and diverse workforce. They accomplished the seemingly impossible by cultivating a culture of open communication, mutual respect, and shared accountability.

Reflection: Are You Increasing Your Influence Through Collaboration?

- **Ask yourself:** Am I prioritizing collaboration to increase my influence and success? Remember that the actual strength of leadership is the ability to inspire and unify others behind a common goal.

Action Step:

This week, prioritize collaborative leadership practices. Accept varied opinions, encourage others to take ownership of their work, and promote open communication. Lead with a collaborative perspective and recognize the importance of shared achievements. By leveraging your impact through collaboration, you may leave a legacy of collective accomplishment and encourage others to reach their full potential.

Maximizing Impact by Leading with Others

"**The function of leadership is to produce more leaders, not more followers.**"
— Ralph Nader

The most effective leaders understand that meaningful impact is made by leading with others, not above them. Leadership is not about having followers; it is about developing and empowering other leaders to take the vision forward. When leaders shift their focus from acquiring authority to multiplying influence via others, they foster a culture of shared leadership that maximizes team effect and assures long-term success.

CHAPTER 20: THE LAW OF INFLUENCE MULTIPLICATION

1. Transition from Top-Down to Shared Leadership

- Traditional top-down leadership is based on a hierarchy, with one person directing and others following. To truly maximize impact, leaders must adopt a shared leadership paradigm in which authority, influence, and accountability are spread among team members. This technique not only improves decision-making but also fosters a sense of responsibility and commitment among team members.
- **Consider:** Are you willing to share leadership with others? Let go of the assumption that you must have all the answers and rely on your team to lead in their areas of expertise.

2. Identify and develop emerging leaders on your team

- Leading alongside others entails actively recognizing and developing emerging leaders. Leaders must be deliberate in identifying potential, providing growth opportunities, and mentoring others to take on leadership responsibilities. Investing in the development of emerging leaders expands your impact and creates a stronger, more capable team.
- **Consider:** Are you providing opportunities for others to develop as leaders? Identify individuals with potential, mentor them, and provide them with the guidance and support they need to succeed.

3. Enable your team to make decisions and take ownership

- One of the most effective strategies to maximize impact is to empower your staff to make decisions and accept responsibility for their job. When leaders transfer responsibility and trust their team members to take initiative, they foster an environment of autonomy and accountability. This empowerment not only boosts confidence but also fosters creativity and a proactive outlook.
- **Consider:** Are you empowering your staff to make decisions and take responsibility? Delegate duties and allow your staff to lead in their areas

of expertise.

4. Promote a collaborative and inclusive culture

- Leading with others necessitates cultivating a culture of collaboration and inclusivity in which all team members feel appreciated and heard. Leaders must prioritize open communication, promote varied viewpoints, and actively solicit feedback from all members. When everyone feels like a valuable member of the team, their dedication and engagement grow.
- **Consider:** Are you creating an inclusive climate within your team? Encourage diversity and collaboration by providing regular chances for open debate and collaborative decision-making.

5. Lead by example and inspire others to lead

- Leading with others entails leading by example. Leaders must model the behaviors and values they wish to see in their teams. This entails displaying honesty, humility, and dedication to the team's common goal. Leaders motivate people to take action, accept responsibility, and embody the same principles by setting a good example.
- **Consider:** Do you provide a good example and inspire others to do the same? Be a leader who exemplifies your values and inspires others to do the same.

Leadership in Action: Nelson Mandela's Collaboration Approach to Leadership

Nelson Mandela's leadership throughout South Africa's transition from apartheid serves as a remarkable example of collaborative leadership. Rather than wanting total control, Mandela aimed to construct a collaborative and inclusive administration. He aimed to empower others, develop togetherness, and establish a common vision for the country's future.

Mandela recognized that long-term change could not be achieved alone. He

CHAPTER 20: THE LAW OF INFLUENCE MULTIPLICATION

actively developed other leaders, encouraged teamwork, and set an example. His leadership style enhanced his influence by emphasizing collaboration and shared accountability.

Reflection: Do You Maximise Your Impact by Leading with Others?

- **Ask yourself:** Am I leading alongside others and empowering them to participate in the leadership journey? Remember that the most effective leaders expand their influence by developing, empowering, and leading alongside others.

Action Step:

This week, prioritize embracing a shared leadership paradigm. Identify and nurture rising leaders on your team, delegate authority, and promote open communication and collaboration. Lead by example and motivate others to take up leadership responsibilities. By maximizing your effect via collaborative leadership, you leave a legacy of empowered and talented leaders who will take the vision forward.

21

Chapter 21: The Law of Legacy Building

Crafting a Lasting Influence

"Leadership is not about being in charge. It is about taking care of those in your charge." — Simon Sinek

Leadership is more than just what you do during your term; it is about the legacy you leave behind. True leaders recognize that their influence extends beyond their current position or organization. They are committed to leaving a legacy that will shape and inspire others long after they are gone. To have a long-term impact, you must be intentional, visionary, and committed to empowering people to carry on the concepts and values you establish.

1. Lead with purpose and clarity

- A clear objective is the foundation for long-term influence. Leaders who understand their "why" and lead with clarity inspire others to organize their efforts around a common goal. Purpose-driven leadership inspires individuals to not just follow, but also to carry out the vision with passion and dedication. When people understand and relate to a leader's mission, the impact is woven into the fabric of the organization or community.

- Ask yourself if you are leading with a clear aim. Reflect on your fundamental mission and ensure that it connects with and inspires those you lead.

2. Concentrate on developing future leaders

- Leaders who have an enduring impact prioritize the development of future leaders. They dedicate their time, energy, and resources to mentoring, coaching, and enabling others to take up leadership responsibilities. This dedication to developing future leaders guarantees that the values, ideas, and vision endure beyond a single individual's term.
- Consider whether you are intentional in developing the next generation of leaders. Create opportunities for advancement, mentor rising leaders, and encourage them to take on new tasks.

3. Model Integrity and Consistency in Leadership

- Integrity is an essential component of long-term influence. Leaders who demonstrate honesty, integrity, and consistency gain the trust and respect of those they serve. This trust, in turn, provides a firm platform for long-term success. Leaders who model integrity provide an example for others to follow, fostering an ethical and values-based leadership culture.
- **Reflect:** Do you lead with integrity and consistency? Strive to be a leader who embodies the qualities you want to see in others.

4. Prioritise relationships over achievements

- Leaders who have a long-term influence recognize that it is more than just getting goals; it is also about the relationships they form along the journey. Leaders foster a culture of loyalty, commitment, and mutual respect by putting people ahead of plaudits and focusing on their teams' well-being. These relationships serve as the foundation for long-term

influence.
- **Consider this:** Do you place equal value on relationships as you do on results? Take the effort to build deep relationships with people you lead, and show real concern and appreciation for their contributions.

5. Foster a culture of empowerment and accountability

- Lasting influence is more than simply individual leadership; it is about building a culture that outlasts any single person. Leaders must prioritize empowering their teams, instilling a sense of ownership, and developing a culture of accountability. When individuals are empowered and held accountable, they become mission stewards and vision advocates.
- Consider whether you are building a culture of empowerment and accountability. Encourage autonomy, delegate responsibility, and hold individuals responsible for common ideals and goals.

Leadership in Action: Mahatma Gandhi's Legacy

Mahatma Gandhi's leadership exemplifies how to create long-term impact. His dedication to nonviolent resistance, social justice, and human dignity made a lasting impression on the world. Gandhi's leadership was defined not by his position or authority, but by his unwavering devotion to his principles and ability to inspire millions to follow them.

Gandhi's influence lasted well beyond his lifetime because he prioritized imparting ideals, encouraging others to lead, and establishing a movement founded on common purpose and honesty. His legacy continues to inspire individuals around the world to lead with courage, compassion, and justice.

Reflection: Are You Creating a Lasting Influence?

Ask yourself: Am I committed to leaving a lasting influence through my leadership? Remember that true influence is measured not by titles or awards, but by the impact you have on the lives of people.

Action Step:

This week, prioritize leaving a lasting impact through your actions. Clarify your goal, invest in future leaders, and demonstrate integrity in your activities. Prioritise connections, foster an environment of empowerment and accountability, and lead to leave a positive and lasting influence. Your influence extends beyond your term, living on in the hearts and minds of the people you inspire.

Building Systems and Succession Planning

"A leader's lasting value is measured by succession." — John C. Maxwell

Great leadership is about setting the framework for long-term influence, not just short-term achievement. One of a leader's most important roles is to create processes that assure continuity and progress even after they leave. Succession planning is an important element of this process since it prepares people to take on leadership responsibilities while still upholding the organization's goals, values, and vision.

1. Create systems that sustain success

- The best leaders understand that their efficacy is not determined by their continual presence, but by the mechanisms they create. Systems give stability, structure, and efficiency, allowing operations to continue uninterrupted even when leadership changes. This includes creating clear communication routes, establishing protocols, and outlining roles and duties.
- Consider whether you are creating mechanisms that will continue to succeed even if you are not present. Consider the processes that must be in place to maintain continuity and stability.

2. Identify and prepare potential successors

- Identification of potential leaders within your team and active preparation for future positions is a critical component of succession planning. Leaders must recognize developing talent and support their development through mentorship, training, and hands-on experience. The goal is not merely to build leaders who can take charge, but also to cultivate leaders who can propel the organization to new heights.
- **Consider:** Are you intentional in identifying and developing future leaders? Focus on developing strategies and opportunities for those with leadership potential.

3. Communicate your vision and core values

- When leaders change, their vision and key principles must remain intact. Effective leaders communicate these fundamental characteristics effectively and consistently, ensuring that all employees understand the organization's mission and guiding principles. By repeating the vision and principles, leaders foster a common feeling of purpose that lasts beyond their tenure.
- **Reflect:** Do you constantly communicate the vision and fundamental principles to your team? Ensure that these aspects are integrated into your organization's culture and processes.

4. Develop a culture of collaboration and innovation

- To be sustainable, systems must be adaptive. Leaders should build a collaborative and innovative culture, encouraging their people to continuously improve processes and devise inventive solutions to problems. A collaborative environment enables system refinement and evolution, making them more adaptable to change.
- Consider whether you encourage collaboration and innovation among your team members. Make room for open communication and collabora-

tive problem-solving to strengthen and adjust your systems.

5. Create a transparent succession plan

- Succession planning should be open and inclusive. Leaders must explain the importance of planning for the future and actively involve important stakeholders. A well-developed and well-communicated succession plan facilitates a smooth transition of leadership and builds trust in the organization's stability.
- Consider whether you have a clear and transparent succession strategy in place. Engage your team in talks regarding leadership continuity, and be upfront about the process with everyone engaged.

Leadership in Action: Steve Jobs and Apple's Succession Planning.

One of the most well-known examples of succession planning is Steve Jobs' strategy at Apple. Recognizing that his health was deteriorating, Jobs made conscious steps to ensure that Apple's success continued after his departure. He identified Tim Cook as his successor, gave him more responsibility, and prepared the company for a leadership transfer.

Jobs also emphasized the significance of Apple's mission and basic principles, making certain that they were thoroughly embedded in the company's culture. This planned succession planning enabled Apple to prosper despite a substantial leadership turnover, highlighting the importance of planning for the future.

Reflection: Are you establishing systems and planning for succession?

Consider whether you are developing long-term systems and actively preparing others to take over leadership. Remember, effective leaders build frameworks that last and invest in future leaders to carry the vision forward.

Action Step:

This week, concentrate on establishing systems and planning for succession. Identify areas where you may improve consistency and structure, and consider the methods required for long-term success. Identify prospective successors on your team, give them with opportunity for growth, and clearly convey the vision and values. By developing sustainable processes and preparing future leaders, you build the groundwork for a long-lasting and meaningful legacy.

22

Conclusion

The Lifelong Journey of Leadership Mastery

Leadership is not a destination; it's a journey of continuous growth, learning, and self-reflection. The principles outlined in this book are not quick fixes or shortcuts to success. They are the enduring laws that guide leaders in every season, challenge, and opportunity.

As you apply these laws, remember that true leadership is not about accumulating followers it's about creating a legacy of empowered individuals who carry the vision forward. Embrace the lifelong commitment to developing yourself and those around you, knowing that every step you take towards leadership mastery is a step towards leaving a lasting impact.

You now have the tools to lead with purpose, clarity, and integrity. But the journey doesn't end here; it begins anew every day as you choose to lead by example, inspire others, and stay true to your values. Continue to challenge yourself, refine your skills, and uplift those you lead.

Leadership is a lifelong calling—answer it with courage and dedication.

www.ingramcontent.com/pod-product-compliance
Lightning Source LLC
Chambersburg PA
CBHW032211220526
45472CB00018B/830